BEGINNING GAME
LEVEL DESIGN

JOHN FEIL
MARC SCATTERGOOD

THOMSON
───────*───────
COURSE TECHNOLOGY
Professional ■ Trade ■ Reference

Figure 1.1 *City of Heroes* ©Cryptic Studios, Inc. *City of Heroes* is a trademark of Cryptic Studios, Inc. and NCsoft Corporation. NCsoft is a trademark of NCsoft Corporation.

Figure 1.2 *Warcraft 3* ©2002 Blizzard Entertainment. All rights reserved. Warcraft and Blizzard Entertainment are trademarks or registered trademarks of Blizzard Entertainment in the U.S. and/or other countries.

Figure 1.3 Deus Ex ©Ion Storm. Deus Ex, Ion Storm, and the Ion Storm logo are trademarks of Ion Storm.

Far Cry, Sandbox, Ubisoft, and the Ubisoft logo are trademarks of Ubisoft Entertainment in the U.S. and/or other countries.

Microsoft, Xbox, and the Xbox logos are either registered trademarks or trademarks of Microsoft Corporation in the U.S. and/or other countries. All rights reserved.

Neverwinter Nights is a trademark of BioWare Corp.

All other trademarks are the property of their respective owners.

Important: Thomson Course Technology PTR cannot provide software support. Please contact the appropriate software manufacturer's technical support line or Web site for assistance.

Thomson Course Technology PTR and the authors have attempted throughout this book to distinguish proprietary trademarks from descriptive terms by following the capitalization style used by the manufacturer.

Information contained in this book has been obtained by Thomson Course Technology PTR from sources believed to be reliable. However, because of the possibility of human or mechanical error by our sources, Thomson Course Technology PTR, or others, the Publisher does not guarantee the accuracy, adequacy, or completeness of any information and is not responsible for any errors or omissions or the results obtained from use of such information. Readers should be particularly aware of the fact that the Internet is an ever-changing entity. Some facts may have changed since this book went to press.

Educational facilities, companies, and organizations interested in multiple copies or licensing of this book should contact the publisher for quantity discount information. Training manuals, CD-ROMs, and portions of this book are also available individually or can be tailored for specific needs.

ISBN: 1-59200-434-2
Library of Congress Catalog Card Number: 2004111221
Printed in the United States of America
05 06 07 08 BH 10 9 8 7 6 5 4 3 2 1

Thomson Course Technology PTR,
a division of Thomson Course Technology
25 Thomson Place
Boston, MA 02210
http://www.courseptr.com

Publisher and General Manager:
Stacy L. Hiquet

Associate Director of Marketing:
Sarah O'Donnell

Marketing Manager:
Heather Hurley

Manager of Editorial Services:
Heather Talbot

Acquisitions Editor:
Mitzi Koontz

Senior Editor:
Mark Garvey

Marketing Coordinator:
Jordan Casey

Project Editors:
Sean Medlock and Jenny Davidson

Development Editor/Technical Reviewer:
Jonathan Harbour

PTR Editorial Services Coordinator:
Elizabeth Furbish

Copy Editor:
Gene Redding

Interior Layout Tech:
Shawn Morningstar

Cover Designer:
Mike Tanamachi

CD-ROM Producer:
Brandon Penticuff

Indexer:
Sharon Shock

Proofreader:
Sara Gullion

I'd like to dedicate this book to my wife and daughter, Jean and Sylvana, who had to spend many, many Daddyless weekends while I wrote this book.

—John Feil

For my wife, Stacie, a very talented author in her own right, for being my support, my personal editor, and my sounding board through this process.

—Marc Scattergood

ACKNOWLEDGMENTS

John Feil

The number of people who have helped me learn and grow and write this book are many. I'd like to thank the Thompson crew, especially Sean , Jenny, Mitzi, and Brandon, for all their help in getting this book out the door. I'd like to thank Marc Scattergood, who came in to write when time got tight. I'd also like to thank Bob Bates for all his help, and Warren Spector for his fine sense of humor. Finally, I'd like to thank this random list of people, who have in some way contributed to my knowledge over the years: Gary Gygax, Todd Nord, Dave Hanifan, Tom Brundige, Rick Andres, Jeff Pipes, Chad Walter, Chris Seeman, Aaron Young, Chuck McFadden, Duncan Brown, Reed Knight, Quentin Westcott, Tim Longo, Rich Davis, Tony Iuppa, John Christian Vanover, and Jason Della Rocca.

Marc Scattergood

Thanks to my wife, Stacie, for putting up with my 12 hour days at work, only to come home and spend another 6 hours in front of my computer, writing.

To John Feil, for being a mentor and a friend, and for including me in this chance to share the knowledge we've gleaned over the years.

I'd also like to acknowledge the *Mythica* team, spread to the four winds as they are, the Sigil Games Online team, who I hope to continue learning from for years to come, and all the friends and co-workers I had in Microsoft Game Studios for their friendship, their shared knowledge and experience, and for helping me strive towards something greater than myself.

ABOUT THE AUTHORS

JOHN FEIL is a game industry veteran whose duties have spanned from quality assurance, to technical writing, and finally to level designer and designer. He's worked on such titles as *Star Wars: Jedi Starfighter* and Microsoft's new Xbox racing game, *Forza*, and is currently a member of the board of directors for the International Game Developer's Association (IGDA).

MARC SCATTERGOOD has been working in the games industry since 1998. In that time he has worked in a quality assurance and operations capacity, as well as level and game design more recently. His shipped titles include *Asheron's Call*, *Sudeki*, and *Zoo Tycoon 2*. Most of that time was spent with Microsoft Game Studios.

He currently is a game designer for Sigil Games Online on the upcoming MMOG, *Vanguard*, and was previously working on the now cancelled MMOG, *Mythica*, as a level designer. He currently resides in Southern California.

CONTENTS AT A GLANCE

Contents

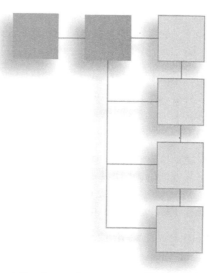

INTRODUCTION

Welcome to *Beginning Game Level Design*, the book that finally makes sense of low-carb diets and whether aliens did indeed seed the planet with humanity. Or maybe that's my other book, *Low-Carb Diets and Alien Conspiracy Theories for Blockheads*. This book is about creating great mods or levels to impress and bring joy to your fellow gamers.

If you've picked up this book, you're probably someone interested in making computer or video games, have some experience playing those games, and hate being talked down to like some ten-year-old child raised by sloths. However, this book is for beginners, so I'm going to take it slow.

I've been a level designer for about 6 years, making games for the PC, the PS2, the N64, and the Xbox. One of the problems I constantly encounter is people asking me what I actually do for a living. I've found that an "I make computer games" satisfies most, but, for more inquisitive folks (like your mom), some deeper explanation is usually required. My funny answer that usually doesn't work is when I explain level design as a process not unlike making macaroni paintings. A mom will instantly know what a macaroni painting is, and will get this reference, because she probably has a couple of these hideous things stored somewhere in her house that her kids made in 2nd grade. People without kids usually look at me like I'm stupid.

Anyway, level design is like making a macaroni painting. A macaroni painting is where a highly adept individual, most likely a child of eight or an elderly woman reading instructions in a lady's crafting magazine, tries to create an image on a piece of paper by gluing pieces of macaroni to it. In this process, the craftsman doesn't make the macaroni, or the paper, or even the glue they use to haphazardly adhere the macaroni to the paper. However, by using these components, they create art. Or, at least, they try to.

Level designers do much the same thing. Level designers don't create the models or textures or characters or even the source code of a game, but by arranging these elements piece by piece, they create fun. Or, at least, they try to.

In this book, I'll show you the basics of how to build a good level or mod. I'll go over basic paper design, creating spaces and architecture, placing units and scripting their behavior, and other areas of expertise you'll need to create a great level. I'll then have some suggested projects at the end of each chapter for helping you directly use the information I just covered.

Throughout the book, I'll be showing you, step by step, the making of a level with Sandbox, a level editor that comes with Crytech Software's excellent game, *Far Cry*. If you have this game, you can use the CD that comes with it to open up the levels I made and see, in color, what we've done at each step.

However, do not fear if you don't have *Far Cry*. This book specifically has been written so that all the lessons within can be applied to just about any toolset or editor.

Who This Book Is For

This book is for people interested in learning the skills to be a level designer. The book covers the very basics, and moves to some fairly advanced topics. However, because of the enormous amount of level editing tools available to the public, this book will deal with general information, rather than specific information on how to build levels in toolsets such as the UnrealEd editor for Epic's *Unreal* game series, or the *Warcraft 3* editor available with Blizzard's *Real-Time Strategy* (RTS) game. *This book should be considered a companion guide to help you master the tool of your choice.* For more specific information about the mechanics of these tools, there are many Web sites that deal specifically with that subject.

How This Book Is Organized

This book is organized in a linear fashion, covering the normal progression of building a level. Step by step, we'll examine the tasks a designer goes through in order to make a mod or a level.

Chapter 1: Basics of Game Design. This chapter will go over the fundamentals of game design. You'll learn about things like power, challenges, and pacing, as well as learn some of the fundamental ways to start approaching your own designs to make them even better.

Chapter 2: Paper Design. You'll go further into designing your own game, learning how to come up with ideas, and how to test them to see if they're good. We'll follow up with how to get those ideas down on paper and how to write a good design document.

Chapter 3: Building Terrain. This chapter will get the ground under your feet by teaching you how to make, texture, and populate terrain in your levels. We'll also cover some strategic uses of terrain and how to get the most gameplay out of appropriate landscaping.

Chapter 4: Building Architecture and Spaces. You'll learn how to plan and build different buildings in this chapter. We'll cover some basic strategy and gameplay elements here, as well.

Chapter 5: Lighting and Atmospheric Effects. We'll cover lighting, fog, particle effects, and ambient audio in this chapter, covering how to use each effect to further enhance the mood of your level.

Chapter 6: Placing Encounters. You'll learn about the different things you can place in a level that the player can interact with. You'll learn about puzzles and encounters, as well as how to place them so that you can maximize the player's fun.

Chapter 7: Breathing Life Into Your Levels. In this chapter, you'll learn some basic information about how scripting can bring your levels to life. We'll cover some of the different languages you can use, and talk about things like setting up patrol patterns and setting up quests.

Chapter 8: Dialogue and Story. You'll learn the basics of how to write solid dialogue and storylines for your game. We'll also cover voiceline audio and how to use story and dialogue to enhance your player's gaming experience.

Chapter 9: Polishing. Your level is done! Now what? In this chapter, we'll cover things like bug finding, ambiance touch-ups, and publishing your level for everyone to see.

Chapter 10: Specific Genres. We'll get in depth to give you tips on how to design for specific genres, like first-person shooters, real-time strategy games, and Internet puzzle games.

On Your Own

Your first project is to create a macaroni painting. Get some heavy cardstock paper, a glue stick or some regular white glue, and a bag or two of salad or elbow macaroni. (Advanced users may use rotini or bow-shaped macaroni for extra flavor.) Using these materials, try to create your favorite game character. Extra credit if the portrait is of the student's favorite game designer, such as Warren Spector or Sid Meyer. After you are done, present the macaroni painting to your mom in a futile attempt to bridge the generation gap.

Tip

Gluing small magnets to the back of your masterpiece will help when applying it to a metal surface, such as a refrigerator.

My rendition of Warren Spector in macaroni, spaghetti, and those little stars that are so good in soup. I call it "Spector La Pasta".

Lesson Learned: Enjoy these tools while you can. Macaroni and glue don't crash on you after 4 hours of work.

Once again, welcome to *Beginning Game Level Design*! You'll be losing weight and seeing extraterrestrials in no time!

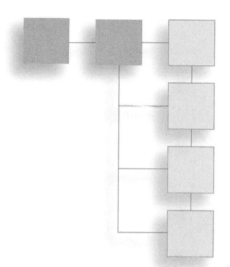

CHAPTER 1

THE BASICS OF GAME DESIGN

Building games is one of the most challenging and rewarding experiences I can think of. Taking pure imagination and making it come alive is absolutely addictive—a creative process so immersive and consuming that you'll start craving it when you haven't done it for too long. Some people think the fun is in playing the game, but, for a few special people, creating and building the environments in which other people play causes mere gameplaying to pale in comparison. If you're reading this book, you are probably one of those special people who have that compulsion to create, and, with your creation, entertain.

Designing your game is the first step on your journey toward bringing your dream to life. Remember, many designers have come before you and failed to deliver. The game design world is like an iceberg: Only a small number of successes have peaked above the frigid water to shine in the sun. These successes are what happens when a great design meets a great team. The rest lurk in an underwater graveyard, rotting slowly in the company of a million other badly designed failures.

To avoid this watery fate, you'll have to be smart, imaginative, tenacious, and driven. You'll need to take a look at those successes and pick them apart like a scavenger bird, ripping out their guts to learn how they managed to get on top of the heap. You can learn from the failures as well, stripping them of their once-bright promises and glinting hype to peer at their ugly, ill-conceived gameplay so you can say to yourself, "I will not follow this path!"

In this chapter, you'll learn the following:

- The basic knowledge you need to begin designing a game
- How to empower the player
- System design
- Different forms of challenges and how to build them
- Pacing and flow
- The beginning, middle, and ending of a game
- Some tips on how to make your games better

The "Fun"damentals

Making games can be a humongous power trip. Having the ability to create what can amount to rat mazes for humans can lead some designers to grow egos the size of a large continent. They lose sight of the core fundamental, which is that games are about one thing: *entertaining people*. This is the first and most important thing to think about when you're making any kind of game, whether it's a teensy mod or a huge, 250-hour RPG. In making a game, you become an entertainer, not a puppet master bent on world domination. As such, your primary concern should be the happiness of your audience and not satisfying your unfulfilled need to punish those who annoy you. You have to make your game fun.

Fun

Fun is the first thing people think about when they hear the word "game." Fun is a simple word, easy to spell, and everyone agrees on what it means. However, the things that people consider fun are as individual as fingerprints. Some people might like hang-gliding, some enjoy going to the mall, some enjoy watching sports, and some enjoy data-entry jobs. Although two people might agree that something is fun, if you get a group of 10 people together, you'll start having problems.

Games are supposed to be fun. People expect them to be sources of entertainment and delight, a source of diversion to distract them from a less-than-perfect existence. The game industry employs thousands of testers and spends millions of dollars a year in market research, trying to determine what people think is fun. So far, no one has really narrowed it down enough to create a magical "fun" formula that guarantees success time after time.

As a future level designer, you'll want to make your levels fun. Although you might not be able to please everybody, there are some ways to hedge your bets.

Know Your Audience

Unless you're making mods that only you are going to play, you'll be making your game for other people. These people will have definite opinions as to what is and isn't fun, and they'll completely pass you over if you don't consider those opinions when making your game. Knowing your audience can be an easy task if you're making a game that isn't exceptionally innovative, such as a first-person shooter (FPS) or a real-time strategy game (RTS). The further you get from the accepted genres, the harder it will be to find your audience. There are exceptions, of course. Sometimes companies create a genre out of whole cloth, much like Maxis did with their wildly successful game *The Sims*.

To *know* your audience, you have to *find* them. Again, it can be pretty simple to find your audience if you're making a game that belongs to an established genre, especially if that genre has an online multiplayer component to it. You can frequent Internet message boards and chat rooms dedicated to games similar to the type of game you want to design to see the opinions of people who play the games like the one you want to create.

Another good place to find people talking about what they like and dislike about games are game review sites and magazines, like Gamespy.com and *Computer Gaming World* magazine. One site that I'd recommend is Gamerankings.com. It's a portal site that gathers links to all kinds of game reviews. You'll be able to find as many opinions on what's good and what's bad as you can handle.

Once you find your audience, pay attention to what they like and what they don't like. This will give you tremendous insight into what to do and what *not* to do when designing your game.

A word of warning: As you start looking for opinions on message boards and chats, remember Sturgeon's law: 99% of everything is crap. For many, the only reason to write anything about a game, positive or negative, is because they have very strong feelings about it. They might not be looking at the game in the most balanced way. A lot of game reviewers can also let their feelings get away from them. Remember, these people are trying to describe why a game is or isn't "fun," and "fun" is a slippery thing to define. Always keep your own counsel, and when you read something that seems highly emotional, try to get what you can from it and move on to the next opinion. Remember, you're trying to make a game that *many* people will enjoy, not just one or two.

Know Your Genre

Just as it's important to know who your audience is, you need to know the games that your own game will be competing with. Not just so you don't unconsciously copy another game developer's work, but to learn what players *expect* from your genre.

Tip

What players expect from your game is perhaps the deciding factor in whether it will be a success or a failure. If you meet the players' expectations, or even exceed them (in a positive way, of course), your game will be a hit. If you fail to meet the players' expectations, well… Welcome to Nowheresville, baby. Population: You.

Expectations are usually generated well before players pick up your game. They'll be influenced by the scanty information you provide on your Web site, the possibly false information generated in online or magazine previews, any marketing you may do, the box your game comes in, and even the name of your game. And, most annoyingly, they'll be influenced by pure conjecture generated by word of mouth. The more your audience's expectations get out of hand, the more disappointed they'll be when they find out that your game *doesn't* actually allow them to match Captain Kirk against Darth Vader in a duel to the death.

It's important to know your genre, and what that genre has given its fans so far. Consider first-person shooters (FPS) games on the PC. Currently, every single FPS uses the W, A, S, and D keys for major movement control. The W key moves you forward, the S key moves you backward, and the A and D keys strafe, keeping you facing forward while moving side-to-side like a crab. Players now expect that key configuration when they sit down in front of any new FPS, and woe to the plucky game company that tries to do it "a better way."

When you're making your game, you need to find all these standardizations that have become associated with your chosen genre. It's not just control configurations, either. A boss at the end of each level is a cliché that a lot of players expect. In an RTS, starting a level near needed resources is expected.

You also need to know the taboos. Jumping puzzles aren't very popular in first-person shooters. Random disasters aren't appreciated in *any* game. Each genre and even each console and the PC have their own "thou shalt nots" associated with them. PC gamers, for instance, hate save points, and like to save anywhere. Console players don't mind as much. The white and black buttons on the XBox controller are hard to get at. By studying games and reading reviews, you can get a good idea of what drives players crazy and what they like.

You should also know your genre well enough to know what sorts of things it could do better. Although some of the mechanics may be set in stone, others might be more pliable. If you can find and improve the things that need improving, or change the things that won't alienate the player, you're on the way to making a great game.

Know Yourself

This may sound a little philosophical, but in order to make a fun game, you truly need to know *yourself*. Or at least you need to know what you think is fun about games. You'll never truly know your audience enough to predict what every single one of them will think is fun. However, you do know what *you* think is fun. When playing a game, whether yours or someone else's, try to notice when you are having a good time. If you can pause, do so and ask yourself what you just did that caused that big smile on your face.

The next step is figuring out why what happened was so fun. Is it because of the way your character moves? Is it because of the rewards you're getting? The victories you're achieving? The cool dialogue? The other players in the game? The intriguing puzzles? The challenge of it all?

You need to find that root, identify it, and really look at it hard. Then, you need to figure out how to implement it in your own game. If you can do this, you're ahead of the pack. Many people can't tell why they're having fun, and if you quiz them about it, they'll give you fairly vague answers that can change each time you ask them. Knowing yourself, and being able to objectively identify the core reason why you feel that a game feature is or isn't fun, is essential to making fun games for other people.

Empowering the Player

Tim Schafer, the designer behind such games as *Grim Fandango* and *Full Throttle*, once noted that all games are about wish fulfillment. When you play a game, you're putting yourself into a fictional scenario that you wish you could experience in real life, at least in general terms. You can be a mighty general in chess, a tough, sarcastic biker in *Full Throttle*, or a powerful dwarven paladin in Blizzard's *World of Warcraft* game.

This is a good point. When you design a game, you want to immerse the player in a role that he thinks is fun and cool. As they say about writing good fiction: "Take me to a place I've never been, make me something I could never be, and let me do things I could never do."

However, I like to boil this down a little more than that. I think that the root of fun in most games has to do with power. When a player feels empowered, achieves some level of competence that was formerly beyond him, that's when he starts having fun.

Empowering the player is pretty easy to do in modern video games. In fact, it's hard not to give the player *too much* power! You can give him super-strength, armies of crack soldiers to command, or even power over life and death itself. He can survive deadly ninja attacks, falls from great heights, or scathing verbal assaults from salty pirates. Game developers can create any conceivable world and make the player its god.

For some players, being a god is the pinnacle of fun. For others, just being a tad more competent than they are in real life brings the most enjoyment. Once again, this goes back to knowing your player and your genre. Knowing how to properly balance your game so that the player has as much of a challenge as he wants, without making it too easy or too hard, is one of the many balancing acts you'll have to face.

A Small Lesson on the Nature of Power

Power, by definition, is the ability or official capacity to exercise control. By understanding the nature of power, and which types of power appeal to which types of players, you can begin to fine-tune your game design technique.

There are three types of power: creative, destructive, and manipulative.

Creative Power

Having creative power allows you to bring something into existence that wasn't there previously, usually by combining separate, already existing objects or concepts. You can create a chair, a meal, or a relationship. Building games, like *Sim City* and *RollerCoaster Tycoon*, focus a lot on this type of power.

Many hobbies and professions revolve around this type of power, from model building and painting to manufacturing cars and game design. Creative power brings with it a sense of accomplishment that is extremely rewarding. Games that focus on creative power are generally considered "toy" types of games because they are more about play than about competition.

Most creative games have two aspects to them, a building aspect and a reward aspect. The building aspect usually concerns itself with giving the player a toolset that allows the player to create whatever he wants given his building materials. An example would be a building game based on Lincoln Logs. The player can use the toolset to create buildings and constructs out of an endless supply of virtual Lincoln Logs: giant log skyscrapers, log statues of famous rock stars, log museums, etc. The reward aspect of the game would issue challenges to the player, such as "build a log International House of Pancakes that seats 100 log citizens with as few logs as possible" and rewards him when the challenge is completed.

There is a large, vocal audience out there that loves creating. However, this type of gameplay is usually complex and time consuming, and can turn off players who want instant gratification.

Destructive Power

Destructive power is the ability to uncreate or radically alter the state of something until it no longer resembles its original form. You can destroy just about anything: civilizations, rhinos, or ideas. Games like *Serious Sam*, *Space Invaders*, and other shooter-style games primarily focus on destruction.

Games that center on destruction are the most satisfying in an immediate sense, and thus are the quickest to empower. Destruction, at least in western culture, is also associated with winning, as this quote from the movie *Apocalypse Now* suggests:

> **Robert Duvall, Apocalypse Now (1979):** *You smell that? Do you smell that? Napalm, son. Nothing else in the world smells like that. I love the smell of napalm in the morning. You know, one time we had a hill bombed, for twelve hours. When it was all over I walked up. We didn't find one of 'em, not one stinkin' body. The smell, you know that gasoline smell, the whole hill. Smelled like... victory. Someday this war's gonna end...*

Erasing all existence of the things and people that annoy and anger in order to "win" drives the nihilistic pleasure that players find in games of destruction and anarchy. Probably not something we want to remind ourselves of very often, but it's a part of human nature that readily becomes apparent when given large weapons and a sense of unaccountability.

Games that focus on this type of power also have the quickest gameplay, with the shallowest learning curve. Players can boot up the game, learn the mechanics, and accomplish something very quickly, making this type of game the friendliest for people with a limited amount of time or short attention spans.

Manipulative Power

Manipulative power allows you to control other things. (It could be argued that this is the only real type of power, but for this discussion, the three types make more sense.) Manipulative power is present in all games. A player can control armies in *Command & Conquer*, control how Lara Croft moves in *Tomb Raider*, or control the falling blocks in *Tetris*.

Manipulative power is the most subtle power, and its correct use rewards the player by making him feel clever and proud of that cleverness. Giving the player the power to manipulate also allows the player to immerse himself in your game, as your game characters become his extensions into your game world.

Games centering on manipulative power usually require the most thought, and can be incredibly complex. Depending on their complexity, they can be short or long experiences: a game of *Tetris* can be short, but a game of *Civilization* can take quite a long time.

The Flow of Power

To be complete, we should also consider the flow of power. In any contest, there comes a point where you have power over your opponent, or your opponent has power over you. If I jump from a step stool, I have the ability to land safely. I've triumphed over the adverse effects of falling. If I jump from a cliff, it's more likely that the adverse effects of falling will overcome me. In the game *City of Heroes* (shown in Figure 1.1), I can jump from any height without killing my character (although he does take quite a bit of damage).

All this is part of the complex web of interrelationships between different power systems in a game. The ability to create, destroy, and manipulate often appear in the same game. Each ability can interact with the others, creating interlocking systems.

Figure 1.1 In Cryptic Studio's *City of Heroes*, players triumph over even the irresistible force of gravity!

System Design

When game systems interact with one another, they create other systems of gameplay, sometimes unintentionally. We call this process *emergent gameplay*, as new systems emerge from the ways the old ones combine with each other.

Using this to your advantage is one of the hardest jobs of the game designer. It requires a lot of thought and knowledge to balance systems so that they work well together without creating powerful loopholes or discrepancies.

For level designers, a lot of the game systems will be in place by the time you get to your toolset. Infliction of damage should be balanced with the characters' resistance to damage. The physics of the game, and how they affect the player, should be there as well. However, when you're starting from scratch, you have to think about these things carefully.

Let's say that you decide to make a game where the player can move crates around by pushing them. You want these crates to react to gravity, so they fall when there's no floor under them. Sticking with this idea, you decide that falling crates can cause damage to players and their foes. Suddenly, you've created a network of interlocking systems that allows a player to push crates from heights on top of unsuspecting foes and kill them.

Now, every time you place a crate within the game, you have to consider whether a player can push it to a place where it can be used to overcome a challenge that you intended to be much more difficult than pushing a box over a ledge. You also have to figure out what to do if the player drops the crate on a friend, or on top of some non-player character (NPC) that the player needed to talk to in order to get to the next level.

These sorts of interconnecting systems bring the flavor of real life to a game. However, it's very hard to predict when the player can use these systems to avoid the gameplay you've set out for them.

Gameplay

Gameplay is a catchall word for whatever the player does with your game that's fun. In *Unreal Tournament*, the gameplay is running around and wasting as many competitors as possible. The gameplay in *Warcraft 3* is controlling troops and defeating enemies. There are as many flavors of gameplay as there are games. When you're creating your game, you'll have to identify what your gameplay is and make it as fun as possible.

Challenges

The challenge is usually the central hub of the gameplay. The objective, and the barriers that prevent the player from achieving that objective, are what determine the challenge. By identifying your challenge, you can boil it down until it's pure.

Here are some of the standard challenges:

- **Time Challenge:** The player is allowed only a certain amount of time to complete a task. This is one of the oldest challenges, and in modern games it's usually combined with some other challenge. A simple example is a race that must be run within a certain time. *WarioWare* uses time challenges in every single mini-game it presents the player.

- **Dexterity Challenge:** The player must accomplish some sort of feat that requires dexterity. In modern games, a dexterity challenge might be shooting a target with a pistol. It doesn't need to be about physical dexterity, though. It could be a mental challenge, where the player has to make quick decisions in order to overcome the obstacles he faces.

- **Endurance Challenge:** Sort of the opposite of a timed challenge. Instead of having a limited amount of time to complete a task, an endurance challenge tests how far the player can go before he falters. Older arcade games like *Defender* and *Pac-Man* were endurance challenges.

- **Memory/Knowledge Challenge:** This type of challenge requires the player to know certain facts in order to win. Game shows like *Jeopardy* present this kind of challenge. In video games, usually it means teaching the player some fact, like "baboons really like barbeque chicken pizza," and then making him recall that fact later on in the game, like using a piece of pizza to lure a baboon guard away from the door to the treasure trove of the Baboon God. Other examples include making the player memorize certain button patterns on the controller to execute combination attacks, remember his way through mazes and difficult terrain, or remember which types of keys work in certain types of locks.

- **Cleverness/Logic Challenge:** Somewhat like the knowledge challenge, the cleverness challenge requires the player to figure out a puzzle without having the answer beforehand. An example would be trying to figure out what combination of buttons to press to open a door. Games like *Tomb Raider* and the *Indiana Jones* series include cleverness puzzles.

- **Resource Control Challenge:** Many games use resource control as the challenge. The player is given a certain amount of a resource. He must use that resource to overcome an objective before it runs out. Strategy games like checkers, chess, and *Warcraft* (shown in Figure 1.2) have finite resources that the player must use to win the game.

Figure 1.2 Blizzard Studio's *Warcraft 3* uses resource challenges to make a compelling real-time strategy game.

Designing Challenges

In most games, challenges are combined to make more complex gameplay. A timing challenge can be combined with a dexterity challenge to create a racing game like *Gran Turismo*. A resource control challenge can be combined with a knowledge challenge to create a game like *Scrabble*. Challenges can be combined in just about any configuration.

As always, when you're designing a challenge, let the game's genre be your guide. What kinds of challenges do you find in similar games? If you're a beginner, re-creating the puzzles and challenges that you've seen in other games can be a great learning experience. If you're an advanced designer, you need to know where the bar is set and what you have to surpass in order to be competitive and not derivative.

Be inventive with your challenges. By deconstructing challenges down to their basic parts and then reassembling them in new and different ways, you can make something unique. However, as mentioned before, you shouldn't stray too far from your genre's roots. Putting a text adventure-style puzzle into a deathmatch arena will confuse the player and make it hard for him to immerse himself fully into your game.

Also keep in mind the setting of your game. If you're creating a jungle-based game, the challenges need to fit the jungle theme. Although this can lead to clichés, with all your puzzles seemingly created by the Professor from *Gilligan's Island*, you always want to make the player forget he's playing a game and let him immerse himself as fully as he can.

Another aspect you'll have to keep in mind is the interface of the game. If you're building an FPS and suddenly you want to add RTS-style challenges, such as the player controlling groups of other units to achieve a goal, you'll probably have to include a lot of interface elements that may break the original gameplay you wanted.

For instance, if you want the player to be able to control other units, you'll have to put in functionality for selecting friendly units. You'll need controls that let the player do everything with those units that they could do in a normal RTS, because people have come to expect that level of functionality in an RTS game. The player must be able to tell those units to go to a certain place, stop where they are, attack, stop attacking, or not attack at all. You'll also need controls for selecting enemies, so the player can tell the controlled units who to attack. FPS games usually don't have a good range of sight (the game character, being on his feet, usually can't see very far away), so you may want to allow the player to disassociate himself from his character and see where he wants to send his units. Suddenly, with all of these mechanics, your player can now see into areas that were supposed to be a surprise. Your programmers are cursing your name and have added an extra year to the development time. Your design becomes less and less like the thing you originally built.

Keeping the player's challenges within the scope of your original interface will help you avoid these problems.

The placement of challenges is also very important. You want the player to not only see the challenge, but also understand it enough to know the first step in solving it. You definitely don't want your challenge to kill the player before he knows it's even there.

An example of a bad challenge would be a camouflaged pit trap that the player can't see until he falls into it. This leads to a game where the player learns by dying, where he knows the dangers he faces only after they've killed him. Another example of a bad challenge would be a door-opening puzzle where the player must press a button completely out of sight of the door it opens. If the player can't establish a mental link between the puzzle and the solution, he's likely to become frustrated and quit playing your game.

Challenges should always be beatable. This seems obvious, but at times you can inadvertently create challenges that *aren't* beatable. If the player must possess a certain object in order to overcome a challenge, and the object becomes inaccessible, the challenge becomes impossible.

For example, let's say that the player controls the rough and ready adventurer Dirk Badsneeze. In level 2, you've placed a key in a fairly out-of-the-way place, on top of a counter. The player breezes right past the key in level 2 and proceeds to level 3, where he's confronted by a locked door. He needs the key from level 2, which is now inaccessible. Before you can say "gesundheit," Badsneeze is stuck and the player has to restart your game.

Another problem is when, in the process of playing your own game repeatedly, you create a challenge that requires an expertise beyond the level of the average player. This is pretty common because designers and testers, having played the game so many times before, start seeing it as too easy and ratchet up the difficulty of the puzzles. However, when a first-time player tries his hand at the puzzle, it's too difficult and he quits. This effect can also spread to your game's story. The designer may start forgetting that the player doesn't know as much about the game world as he does, so he starts leaving out small bits of information that the player needs in order to make sense of it all.

Challenges, more than anything else in your game, need to be perfected. You'll never create a great challenge on the first try. It takes a lot of tweaking, or iteration, to get it right. Once you've created a challenge, run through it again and again to make sure everything goes off without a hitch. Then, give it to other people and watch how they deal with it. Always try to make your challenges as solid, understandable, and fun as possible.

Once you've created all your challenges, you need to figure out where to place them. In some games, the challenge is constant. *Tetris*, *Space Invaders*, and most other arcade games have constant challenges. More recent games, especially those that revolve around a story or a variety of different goals, have their challenges spaced apart. The player goes from one challenge to the next, resting in-between. This pattern of challenge/rest/challenge determines the pacing and flow of your game.

Pacing and Flow

The designer usually looks at the game as a whole and doesn't think too much about the individual challenges the player will face on a minute-by-minute basis. However, as a level designer, you'll be concerned about what the player will face every moment he spends in your level.

Game pacing uses challenges and breaks to establish a rhythm and tempo. A well-paced game has a flow to it; tension and relaxation follow one another to draw the player through the game.

This technique is widely understood in the realm of filmmaking, and it's perfectly applicable in game design as well. Action leads to excitement, which isn't sustainable for a very long time. You need to give the player a chance to cool off. A lull after each challenge allows the player to take a break, marshal his resources, and go into the fray once again.

In some games, this rhythm is easy to establish. In older arcade games like *Defender* and *Pac-Man*, the player gets about 5 minutes of gameplay to complete a level, and then a short rest as the next level is loaded. This little break was just as important to making these games compelling as the actual gameplay. In a lot of modern games, levels take a bit longer than 5 minutes, so rest breaks have to be included within each level. In single-player first-person shooters, this break is usually accomplished by not respawning enemies in a certain location. After the player has finished defeating all the enemies in one location, he can remain there and feel somewhat safe as he unwinds briefly. Then he can move to the next encounter. In platform games, the end point of a difficult puzzle or challenge is usually a safe zone where the player can rest for a minute.

Some games, though, use different means to create a rhythm. Most real-time strategy games don't have a rest component until the end of each level, which can sometimes take over an hour! The pacing is in the rhythm of managing each battle and then maintaining the growth of your forces and moving them into position for the next fray. In games like this, having a pause function can help the player generate his own rhythm. However, pausing can also disrupt the player's immersion in the game and make it hard to get back into it.

First Impressions: In the Beginning

The most important part of any game is the first 10 minutes. Unless you make them so compelling that the player can't put down the controls, he'll find it very easy to quit and never touch your game again. After all, he has very little emotional investment and a plethora of other games to choose from.

A good first impression is a pretty tough thing to accomplish. For one thing, whenever a player starts a new game, he enters a new universe. He only has a vague idea of how to do anything, from walking to putting on his clothes to opening a door. This makes the player feel dumb. Remember how the player wants to feel empowered? In the first 10 minutes of a game, even if the player has the power of a god, he'll feel like the biggest idiot on the planet. No one likes that feeling, so you need to make this breaking-in period as quick as possible.

There are a couple of things in your favor. It's likely that your player has played other games, so he'll know which way to hold the controller. If your game uses controls similar to other games in its genre, the player will feel almost comfortable right from the start. If your game is a sequel to or a mod of a game the player has played before, he probably won't feel dumb in the least. This is why sequels are so popular. Players don't have to invest any time in learning a new interface.

The player is also likely to know a little about the setting of your game. If it's sold in a retail store like Electronics Boutique, the player was probably attracted to the packaging. Or maybe he's read some reviews or a brief blurb on a download site, or a friend has recommended the game to him. Whatever makes the player purchase or download your game will also help him get through that deadly first 10 minutes.

However, all this is hardly sufficient if the player still feels stupid or frustrated. As the game designer, you have to teach the player about his new environment, while entertaining him enough to keep him playing.

Most games start with an introductory movie. Although the player doesn't get to interact with this movie, it introduces him to the gameworld and his character's place in it. Generally, this introductory movie is the best-looking thing in the game. The developers know that they need to capture the player, so they throw the whole works at him: flashy explosions, beautiful vistas, scantily clad women, etc. They want the player to think that the rest of the game will be this sweeping and epic.

The introductory movie explains the setting of the game and shows off some of the gameplay that the player will experience, whether it's racing cars, battling aliens, playing a sport, or placing blocks on top of one another. It briefly lays out the story of the game, giving the player enough knowledge that he doesn't feel completely confused when he finally gets to play.

After the introductory movie is over and the player gets to start playing, the designer's next step is to start feeding information to the player. You want him to feel confident about playing this game with something resembling competence.

Note

At this point, you may be thinking, "What about the game manual? Why doesn't the player just read the manual that comes with the game, so I don't have to waste time on expensive CGI movies or training levels?"

Unfortunately, today's players generally don't read manuals. For one thing, they aren't very entertaining. When a player picks up a game, he wants to be entertained as soon as possible, so he skips the boring stuff and jumps right into the gameplay. Also, manuals these days are expected to fit inside a DVD box, which limits them to 15 or 16 pages. Even if you do want to provide an entertaining manual, you'll have a bit of a problem fitting a funny bon mot between the necessary pictures of the controller and the credits pages. (You *do* want your name in the manual, don't you?)

In most games, the solution is a thinly veiled training session. This usually takes the form of a few very basic encounters where the player is taken from simple lesson to simple lesson. Teach him a skill, let him play with it for a bit, and then take him to the next lesson. Teach him what various UI elements do (such as status bars), how to use the UI, and how to use the different menus and what the options on each menu do. Then teach him how to interact with the game, such as combat strategies or the core gameplay itself.

This is actually a powerful, efficient way to teach. However, since you're in that dreaded first 10 minutes, your lessons also have to be *fun*. In many story-based games, these lessons are taught by a non-player character, someone who speaks clearly and is amusing. That way the player is entertained while he practices using the A button to open doors.

During this training, especially in story-based games, you may want to shove a bunch of exposition down the player's throat. "As you know, the Elder Muskrats besieged the town of Dryer in 1528, which was when your grandfather, who was Dryer's greatest smith, created the Tongs of Eldwere when he found getting hot dogs out of boiling water to be too painful…" *Bad idea.* Try to avoid doing too much exposition at once.

If you can make all of this training fun and transparent, those first 10 minutes will fly by. The player will think, "I am *awesome* at this game!" He'll feel like he's discovered some sort of hidden talent he never knew he had until he started playing *your* game.

In the Middle

The middle of your game will contain the bulk of your gameplay. This is where you put all the levels, plot twists, cool items, and everything else you want to stuff into your game.

The most important two concepts for the middle of your game are consistency and growth. Your game world, whether it's a boxing game or a kart racer, has to have an internal consistency. If the player can pick up one vase, he expects to be able to pick up all vases from that point on. Even if the physical laws of your game are nothing like real life—let's say that cats are now frictionless and dogs are superconductors—once the player immerses himself in your world, he'll be very disappointed if he suddenly finds a cat he can't use as a hockey puck.

Consistency is very hard to maintain when you decide to balance your game. For instance, if you're finding it too simple to get through certain parts of your game, you might be tempted to adjust how much damage the enemy's weapons inflict, or to make them harder to hurt.

Even if the change is subtle, players will notice immediately. They might not count how many laser blasts it takes to destroy a Snarg Interceptor, but they'll feel a sense of disempowerment when it suddenly takes four instead of three.

Growth is the second most important concept in most games. As the player progresses through your game, he'll get better at playing it. In today's games, the standard method of keeping the player from getting bored is to ramp up the level of challenge incrementally, keeping him on his toes as he faces greater and greater adversity.

In many games, growth in the player's abilities is aided artificially as the player's character grows more powerful. In many FPS games, the player gets access to more and more powerful weapons and armor as the game goes on. RPGs do this as well, and they also allow character growth, making the character progressively stronger and more resistant to damage. RTS games give access to new units, fighting games unlock new moves, and racing games allow the player to drive better cars.

Throughout a game, the level of difficulty should be incremental. A game that has sudden surges in difficulty can frustrate the player, causing him to quit. A game that suddenly becomes too easy will bore the player, who might move on to something more entertaining. To ensure a gradual increase in difficulty, you need to test the game over and over to make sure it's consistent. Then have other people test it, just to make sure you haven't become blind to your game's weaknesses, or to unforeseen ways of finishing it. Believe me, there will be ways of playing your game that you never imagined, often bypassing much of the content you've slaved over.

The Finale

The end of a game is both the easiest and hardest part to design. It's easy because you no longer have to train the player. He already knows how to play your game as well as can be expected. You don't need to pull your punches anymore, or worry about how you're going to top that last challenge. It's kind of a freeing experience, not having to worry about babying the player along anymore.

It's also hard, because the end needs to be satisfying. The player needs to feel that he has overcome the best you could throw at him. (Which isn't true... but he has to *think* that.) The finale needs to wrap up any plot hooks that might be laying about, all the bad guys who retreated earlier in the game need to show up, and you need to give out any quest items that the player needs before he fights the big bad boss.

Climax and Denouement

There are two parts to an ending: the climax and the denouement (pronounced *day-new-ma*). The climax is the height of excitement, where the plot comes together and resolves itself in a way that's entertaining to the audience. The denouement is the part *after* the climax, where any hanging plot points or clarifications are given. In *Star Wars*, the climax is when Luke Skywalker blows up the Death Star; the denouement is the award ceremony afterward. It's always important to have a denouement in story-based games, so the player doesn't feel like there's something more he should do. The player needs that sense of closure. He needs that final sense of reward, where the game, through its characters, congratulates the player on a job well done, and assures him that they appreciate his efforts. The denouement is when you remind the player how much his character has grown in both power and wisdom, and how that growth has affected his place in the world.

Using the *Star Wars* example, the awards ceremony shows us Luke Skywalker as a changed man. In the beginning, he was a friendless, whiny farm boy whose self-centered world view was focused purely on how tough he had it being a moisture farmer on a nowhere planet. By the end, we see him standing tall, accepting awards with some dignity along with Han Solo and Princess Leia, both of whom had looked at him like he was a backwater idiot earlier in the movie, and now look at him as an equal and a friend. Showing us this growth in the movie helps remind us of all that has happened, and brings to our minds "what comes next?"

The Climax

In the climax, or the finale of the game, you want the player to use all the tricks he's learned. Challenges have to be wide-ranging, allowing the player to demonstrate all the skills he's learned while progressing through your game. You should allow him to use the best weapons, the fastest vehicles, or the coolest martial arts moves. Let him be the master he's trained the whole game to be.

The end challenge has probably been fairly predictable for some time by the climax. The player will have a general idea of whom or what he'll be facing and be raring to go. For this reason, it's usually best to make your climax straightforward, but tough. Don't try to throw in any unexpected gameplay or tricks at this time that you haven't already used. The finale should be the culmination of everything that has come before, not a step in a new direction.

Finishing a good finale should leave the player sweaty and joyful. He has achieved victory after a hard-fought battle. An easy success here would be disappointing to the player.

Unfortunately, this is usually too often the case. In a lot of games, the player has accumulated so much experience and equipment that it becomes hard to defeat him without cheating. There is also a lot of range in what each individual player's abilities are, so it becomes hard to predict exactly how a player might approach your finale.

Once again, playing this battle over and over, in every single way you possibly can, is the way to find those weaknesses and overcome them. The end of your game is often the determining point on how well a player remembers your game, or how well a reviewer scores it. The finale of your game is nearly as important as the beginning in this respect. Make sure your climax is the best it can possibly be.

The Denouement

The end movie is usually created to illustrate the denouement. In order to show the player how much his character has changed, and how the universe has been affected by his deeds within your game, you'll probably plan to include something just as grand or grander than the initial, beginning movie.

Unfortunately, things will probably have conspired against you.

Games change in their making. As your game comes to life, some aspects will have become obviously undoable, and some really nice, new plot events or features will get implemented along the way. This makes the end of the game highly unstable until such time that you've cemented down all of the parts previous to it.

This means that your ending movie will probably be the last thing you want to create, since it needs to incorporate the whole of all that has come before it. Because of this, a lot of pressure in terms of time, money, and resources will build up. You'll be running out of time, running out of money, and running out of people by the end of the project.

It would be easy to just let the whole thing go. To make a short, sorry little movie that barely does justice to your game.

Don't do that! The players who have worked so hard to get through your game should be rewarded. Give them the best ending you can. If your game isn't story-based, like a racing game, save something really nice to give the player after he beats that final opponent. Be creative with it. Just make sure that the end of your game receives all the attention and love that it deserves.

Making Your Game Better

Like any skill, designing games is something you get better at with practice. You'll develop a bag of design tricks that you can draw from: how to make a challenge tougher, how to better pace your game, where a story works and where it doesn't. In this section, I want to share some of the stuff I've learned that has made me a better designer.

Respect the Player

The player is not your enemy. He's your paycheck. He's just as smart as you are, and he has similar goals and dreams. He deserves your respect and thanks.

Show that you respect the player's time by letting him quit your game at any time without losing his place. If possible, don't make him redo things he's already done. Give him as much choice as you can allow (*Deus Ex* is a great example—see Figure 1.3). Let him choose how his character looks, what sex his character is, and how his character deals with the various challenges you present him. Always make your game's rules and laws consistent. The player must know the consequences of failure, and it must be dealt with swiftly so he can start playing again as soon as possible.

There are a thousand more ways to show your respect for the player. Try to do so any way you can.

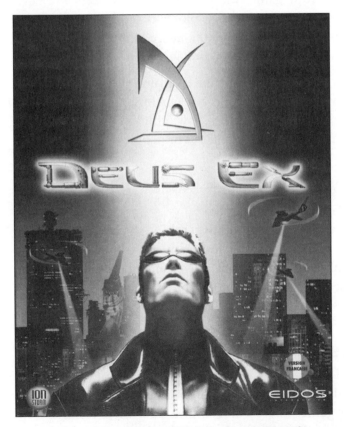

Figure 1.3 Ion Storm's *Deus Ex* shows great respect for the player. The single-player campaign allows for several different play types, which can be combined to customize how the player overcomes the game's many challenges.

Hubris Is the Game-Killer

Game designers often suffer from hubris, or excessive pride and presumption. This is generally the result of the designer forgetting that he is an entertainer, and thus providing a service for others. Instead, he begins to feel that he is an artist, who is allowing others to play in a world of his own design.

You can tell you have hubris if you suffer from the following symptoms:

1. A general dislike or hatred for your audience. You feel as if your players are intellectually stunted children and annoying, unworthy opponents.
2. You easily become upset when you see someone playing your game in a way that you didn't mean it to be played.
3. You begin to take delight in thinking of ways to punish players for doing stupid or objectionable things within your game, like using cheat codes or acting in anti-social ways toward friendly non-player characters.
4. You begin to take bad reviews or insulting internet posts as personal attacks on your character.

Hubris can make you forget to try to make a fun game, and will cause you to be blind to obvious faults within your creations. It will give you easy excuses to salve your ego as you start thinking of anyone who doesn't like your game as a jealous low-brow troglodyte maliciously trying to tear your game down.

Basically, hubris will make you a jerk and a bad game designer.

As I said at the beginning of this chapter, creating games is all about entertaining others. Never forget that. Try to stay above the fray and concentrate on making the best experience you can. *Avoid hubris.*

If *You* Aren't Having Fun, the *Game* Won't Be Fun

You can't make a worthwhile game unless you're having fun doing it. If you dread working on your game, it probably won't be very fun. Even if you do manage to finish it, what's the point?

This isn't to say you have to be giggling with glee through every step in the process, or that you shouldn't take the game seriously. But people tend to be more creative when there's laughter involved. Advertising tycoon David Ogilvy once said, "The best ideas come as jokes. Make your thinking as funny as possible." He also said, "If it doesn't sell, it isn't creative." Fun helps spark creativity, and creativity helps sell your game.

It's Just a Game

Finally, the last thing to remember is that you shouldn't sacrifice relationships with your family or friends because of a game. It's easy to get lost in the work and spend long hours on it, ignoring the people you care about in the process. Creating games is *not* a higher calling. Your game won't save any lives. It won't bring about a social upheaval that brings peace to the world. You're entertaining people. That's important, but not as important as your own life. Don't squander your relationships so somebody you'll never meet can have a few hours of diversion.

What You Have Learned

This chapter has taught you the following concepts:

- Games are for entertaining people.
- To come up with clear ideas about what does and doesn't work in games, you should study three things: your audience, other games in your chosen genre, and your own gaming preferences.
- Games should empower their players.
- A game's challenges make up its gameplay.
- Breaking down challenges into their most basic forms allows you to use a mix-and-match method to create new, innovative challenges.
- Give the player rest breaks between challenges. This helps to create a good pace, which keeps him playing your game.
- The first 10 minutes of your game are the most important.
- Consistency and growth are the two main concepts that keep your game interesting and playable.
- At the end of your game, give the player a good sense of closure. Also, reward the player who finishes your game.
- Respect your player.
- Don't fall into an "Us vs. Them" mindset.
- Give your game as much polish as possible, and have fun doing it, but don't forget your family and friends in the process.

Review Questions

(Answers are located in Appendix C)

1. As a game maker, your primary duty is to do what?
2. What are the three types of power?
3. Where can you go to find opinions and thoughts about games so you can find out what works and what doesn't?
4. Name three types of challenges:
5. What is hubris?

On Your Own

1. Go to Gamerankings.com and look for your favorite game. Read the best review, the worst review, and a preview.

   a. Did the preview have any information about the game that was just plain wrong? If so, what was it? Also, how do you think the players felt when they found out this facet of the game wasn't in the final version?

   b. What did the worst review and the best review disagree on? Did you feel one of them was wrong? Why?

2. Pick a game that you've finished and write a mini-review of it. (This shouldn't be the same game that you looked at in the previous exercise.) This mini-review should cover the following:

   a. The game's greatest strengths.

   b. Its greatest weaknesses.

   c. The most compelling moment of that game, the part that you remember best.

   d. The user interface, including which keys or buttons performed which actions, what the screen looked like when you were playing, and what the menu system looked like. Include a paragraph on what they could have done to make it better.

3. Write down five different ideas for games. They can be silly or serious. Using what you know about how games are developed, identify the game that would be the easiest to create, and the one that would be hardest to create.

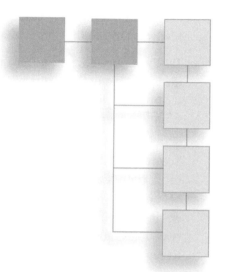

CHAPTER 2

PAPER DESIGN

Every level begins with an idea. Ideas are formed from a variety of things: images, concepts, emotions, and sensory input like taste and smell. All these things are knotted together like a ball of yarn, and if you unravel them, frequently you find they have no center.

Turning an idea into a game is what level designers do. They take ephemeral things and give them form. This means that a good designer must learn how to distill ideas into a solid, definable, workable game.

In this chapter, you'll learn the following:

- How to come up with ideas
- Making sure your ideas are keepers
- How to form those ideas into a design document
- How to make maps that illustrate your ideas

Coming Up With Ideas

I'll bet you already have plenty of ideas about what kinds of games you'd like to make. In many cases, the toolset you use is going to define the kind of game you're going to build. If you're using the UnrealEd toolset, you'll probably be making a variant on the sci-fi FPS. If you're using the *Warcraft 3* toolset, it's likely going to be a fantasy-based real-time strategy map. If you're a professional level designer, the idea will come from the designer of the game, and your ideas might only be small modifications to the grand plan.

If you can't think of a game you'd like to make, or you're looking for fresh ideas, there are a few ways to get the ideas flowing:

- **Talk with your friends.** This is the cheapest and best way to brainstorm game ideas. It's likely that your friends have similar interests, so have a good conversation over pizza about what the heck the game world needs next. This can usually generate a few interesting ideas that you can use to build a mod or game.

- **Scour the Internet.** If you're an amateur looking for some new ideas for a mod, there's a neverending supply of forums on the Web where players from around the world post about what they'd like to see happen in their favorite games. By picking and choosing carefully, you can find an interesting idea or two. These forums have a very low signal-to-noise ratio, however, so you'll need to dig around for the good stuff.

- **Play the game whose toolset you'll be using.** This pretty much goes without saying. If you're planning on doing an *Unreal* mod, play *Unreal Tournament*. After each play session, write down what changes to the game you'd like to see, especially in terms of the environment. (Writing things down is very important, because I guarantee you'll forget otherwise.)

- **Play similar games to the one whose toolset you're using.** Write down all the cool things you see that you'd like to implement in your mod.

Once you have an idea of what kind of game you'd like to make, be sure to think about the following aspects of your game:

- **The player's character.** Who's the main character of your game? Is he a nameless warrior who the player uses as an avatar in a competition, like in an FPS? Or is he a highly developed persona who the player must immerse himself in, such as Max Payne?

- **The environment the game takes place in.** The engine and toolset you're using will steer you toward a specific category, but you'll still have a lot of options as to how to fill in your environment. Will it be a lost temple in an equatorial jungle? A drifting space station filled with radioactive monsters? A huge plate of turkey and mashed potatoes?

- **The people or creatures that populate the environment.** What lives on that plate of turkey and mashed potatoes? Are there friendly sweet potatoes that want to help the player in his quests? Are there evil, radioactive green beans and huge rolling peas that threaten to squash the player at every turn?

- **Is there a plot to the level?** Is there a deliberate sequence of actions that take place during the game?

Once that's done, it's time to look at your idea closely to see how viable it is. Here are a few steps you can take to see if an idea is workable, or if it's one of those balls of yarn I told you about:

- **Write down your game idea.** There's nothing that reveals how needlessly complex and utterly stupid an idea is than putting it down on paper. Ideas are often sublingual. They're images and emotions bundled up into something that *feels* like a great idea. When you try to put an idea into words, your brain has to tear the idea apart and put names to all the concepts it's made of. Very few if any "great ideas" can make it past this phase unaltered. Much of the time, though, this will make you think about the idea enough to start modifying it so that it makes sense. Your idea may not come out as pure as it was when it popped into your mind, but it will be a lot more resistant to criticism.

- **Read what you've written out loud.** This process, although it might feel a little awkward, will reveal weak spots that made it past your mental process of writing it down. Often, your ability to write meaningful prose can suffer when you're excited. Have you ever read an e-mail or Internet post from someone who's obviously very excited and has lost the ability to construct a sentence, creating paragraph after paragraph of indecipherable nonsense filled with logic holes and bad spelling? Do you think the writer *intended* it to be that hard to understand? Reading back your ideas out loud forces you to pay attention to the problems you might have missed in your rush to write them down.

- **Take the core idea you've written down and share it with your friends.** Ask them to describe your mod to you, based on their reading of your idea. You're not asking for their opinion; you're asking them to show where you might have skipped a step or haven't thought out a concept clearly. During this process, it can be very, very hard not to get defensive about your idea and start arguing about what you *really* meant. The point here is that if something is misinterpreted, it means you didn't spell it out as clearly as you thought it was. Write down all the parts that your friend didn't understand or didn't explain well enough to your satisfaction, and then modify your written idea to take those problems into account. I know that this can be a little more work than you thought it was going to be, but if this puts you off, wait until you find out how much work actually *implementing* your idea is.

- **Write a recipe list for what it will take to create your idea in a game or mod.** Is it just a new environment, using all the same characters and weapons the game normally uses? Does it require new characters or weapons? Does it require NPCs to speak to the player or to act in a certain way? Try to make the list as granular (detailed) as possible. It's okay if you don't know how to make the things on the list happen; just write them down. Depending on your experience at making mods or levels, this list will probably cover only 25-60% of all the tasks required to create your level as you've envisioned it.

- **Ask yourself two questions.** Question 1: "Do I have enough time to create all the stuff that I need to implement my idea?" Question 2: "Am I still excited by this idea, now that I understand it completely?" If the answer to either of these is "No," you might want to go back to the drawing board.

At this point, you've created the bones of your first game design document. You rock! You also have a beginning task list, which will be a great help if you lose momentum and start groping blindly for what you need to do next.

Once you've solidified your idea, the next step is to start mapping it out. After all, level and mod design is primarily about creating spaces in which the game is played.

First, research the kinds of areas you want to emulate. This means looking at pictures of existing places, as well as painted landscapes to develop a sense of the architecture or terrain you want to create. Look at pictures of forests, deserts, or mountains that might look similar to the places you are trying to create, or go through books like the excellent *Spectrum Series* (published by Underwood-Fuller) to see some great art detailing imaginary places.

One of the easiest ways to look for pictures is to go to Images.Google.com. This service allows you to search the entire Internet for images related to your keyword. Type in whatever you want: "Blade Runner," "Desert," "Machu Picchu," "Nebraska," whatever, and watch as it brings up hundreds of images that can help you flesh out your terrain. Of course, this is a little hit and miss, and you'll get plenty of images that won't help, but this is always the first place I go for ideas.

Books and magazines are other good places to find images. Your local library is the best place to get research material. Or, if you're like me and you're driven to own your own books rather than borrow them, used book stores are great. Regular bookstores like Borders and Waldenbooks also have books in their bargain racks with lots of interesting photos. Look for books and magazines that focus on what you're trying to build: *National Geographic* has great terrain and outdoor photos, architecture books have photos of unique buildings, and pen-and-paper roleplaying games like Columbia Games' *HarnWorld* line have detailed maps for continents, cities, towns, buildings, and of course, dungeons and the like.

After you've immersed yourself in the theme of your level, get some paper and begin drawing basic maps of the area you'll be creating. This phase is where you nail down the basics of the gameplay and how your environment facilitates that. (We'll further discuss the design of spaces in a future chapter.)

The first thing to consider is the overall goal of the mission you're building. How does the player win? Does he have to kill a boss, open a chest, defeat an enemy army, or create an impressionist painting and sell it to the highest bidder in an auction filled with vampires? If you've written down your game ideas, you've probably answered this question already.

The second thing to consider is which obstacles are preventing the player from achieving his goal. In most popular games, these obstacles are a combination of environment and enemies. The environment separates the player from his goal with locked doors, death traps, maze-like pathways, and so on. Enemies are usually placed in the player's path as moving obstacles that he must overcome.

After considering these two things, draw out the space you're envisioning on paper. Keep it simple at first. Draw the shape of the space you want to use. Once that's done, draw where the player starts and where different obstacles are, including the final obstacle or enemy. Draw any environmental obstacles, like mazes, rivers of lava, walls, gates, doors, and so on.

Some things to keep in mind:

- Levels are innately closed areas. The player will only have a finite amount of room in which to move around. However, players dislike it when they're being forced onto one path. The art of level design is to make players think that they have infinite choices when really they have only a few. Try to give the player choices about the pathways they take.

- Until you're experienced with the game engine you're using, limit the number of enemies your player can fight at once to around 4-5 or fewer. Some engines do better with many enemies, but some don't. Playing the game that your toolset belongs to will give you a good idea of your limit.

- Make notes on the map, detailing where lights may be coming from, what kinds of materials the surfaces are made of (brick, wood, viscous yellow goo), etc.

- Make more notes on the map, spelling out what the player encounters in each area. I usually just number the map and write down this stuff on a separate piece of paper.

Once you're done with this, you probably have a very good mental image of what you want to design. However, for some people, a plain map might not be enough.

For levels that have a strong plot, it's usually good to outline the different characters and events the player encounters during the level. A simple list of characters and the information they give the player will usually suffice. However, when I'm stuck for what needs to happen in a level, I like to draw a comic strip (what the movie people like to call a *storyboard*) that follows the player's adventures in the game. This is actually pretty fun even if you can't draw (I sure can't), and it will probably result in a lot more creativity than you'd get with an outline.

Another way to flesh out a level before designing it is to roleplay through it. In the simplest manner, you can just pretend you're the player going through your level. Try to think of ways you can cheat to get out of overcoming all of the obstacles in your path. Think of all the questions you might ask yourself about the level as you're playing.

The advanced method is to use an actual pen-and-paper roleplaying game (RPG) and run some friends through your level. You'll want to use a flexible RPG whose player characters have abilities roughly equal to those in your game. The advantages of this method are that it reveals a ton of weaknesses in your plans, gives you a lot more ideas to implement, and really firms up your concept of what your level is all about. On the downside, it's a lot of work, and you won't get as much out of it if you're inexperienced at running these sorts of games.

Writing a Design Document

Once you have your idea fleshed out, you might want to create a design document. This document serves several purposes:

- It helps you remember what you want to do.
- It keeps you on track.
- It tells other people working on your level exactly what you want to create, so everyone stays on the same page.

The formatting of a design document is pretty much up to you. It can be paragraph after paragraph of narrative describing the story of the game, or it can be a simple outline of what the player encounters as he goes through the level. The following are some tips on how to make a good game design doc:

- Make it as plain-spoken as possible. Bad or complicated writing can lead to bad assumptions, which can lead to big mistakes.
- Make it as linear as possible. Begin at the beginning, and end at the end. This may seem obvious, but it takes a lot of thought. You need to describe the level in linear terms, even though it's made up of events that can be approached in any order.

- For non-linear action points, such as unrelated encounters that the player can approach in any way, put the descriptions in bullet points:
  - Three Mutant Marsupials lie in wait for the player, hidden behind a eucalyptus tree. Each marsupial has a sharp stick and can kick and claw with its feet.
  - Two Dingos can be found sitting at a low wooden table. On the table is a plate with a single cookie on it. When the player approaches, one Dingo asks the player to help, while the other warns him off. Each Dingo can bite for extreme damage. If the player can find an extra cookie and give it to one of the Dingos, they'll give the player some more ammunition for his rubber-band gun.
  - A pool of quicksand surrounds a life-size cardboard standee of Paul Hogan. The player can rescue it from the quicksand with his whip. Taped to the back is a cookie that he can give to one of the Dingos.
- Make the document as complete as possible. Describe the scenery, the terrain, and any other element that you want present in the game. If you're working with other people, this will help reduce the amount of time you'll spend answering questions.
- Include as many references as you can. Create maps, reference movies, paste in pictures, or do anything else you can to help others visualize what your game will resemble when you're done.
- *Don't* include things like programming tips, marketing strategies, or milestone schedules. This just dilutes your document. Put anything that doesn't have to do with describing your game in different documents.
- If you want to be a real professional, make your document into a Web page. Every level should have its own page, and it should be accessible from every other page. Web documents like this are nice because many people can view them at once, and they're easy to change on a moment's notice.

Creating Maps

A picture is worth a thousand words, and a map is worth even more. A single map can bring a level into focus much more powerfully than any amount of text. Making a map can also reveal weaknesses in your game design and bring into focus the challenges of the game's terrain.

Making a map isn't very hard. A good top-down map will usually suffice to show what's happening, and where. A topographical map, if you can manage it, is also handy for showing elevation differences in terrain (see Figure 2.1).

The following are some tips for making maps:

- Graph paper is the best friend of the mapmaker. If you draw your maps on unlined or single-rule paper, it's harder for readers to judge scale.

- On maps of terrain, try to show major landmarks like mountain ranges, lakes, canyons, outcroppings, and so forth.

- Keep scale consistent. One inch = 100 yards, 10 squares of graph paper = 1 furlong, etc. This will help you (or any 3D artist who's helping you) visualize how big or small the area will be.

- Mark the areas where you plan on staging major encounters. If you want to have wandering encounters (enemies that patrol an area, a traveling salesman going from town to town, etc.), it's good to mark their territory or the path those encounters travel.

- Don't get too meticulous. You just want an abstract of the area. You don't need to draw every single blade of grass.

- If you're marking areas with numbers (traps with a 1, enemies with a 2, etc.), make sure the map has a legend explaining what those numbers mean.

- When you're making blueprints for buildings and rooms, it's handy to use one of the many free home-planning CAD programs on the Web. Even the most rudimentary CAD program can help you keep your map to scale and draw perfect shapes for rooms.

Example: Prospero's Island

In each chapter, I'll be demonstrating some of the skills I'm writing about by creating an example level. You can find materials relating to these examples on the CD-ROM attached to this book.

In this chapter, I'll be coming up with the basic idea of the example and then fleshing it out on paper.

First: The idea. After talking about it with some friends, we decided that there aren't enough Shakespeare-based first-person shooters. After all, who's bloodier than Othello, more vindictive than Hamlet, more murderous than Richard the Third? Obviously, the game industry has completely ignored this gold mine of rights-free intellectual property. I figure that the time has come for an FPS based around the Shakespeare play *The Tempest*.

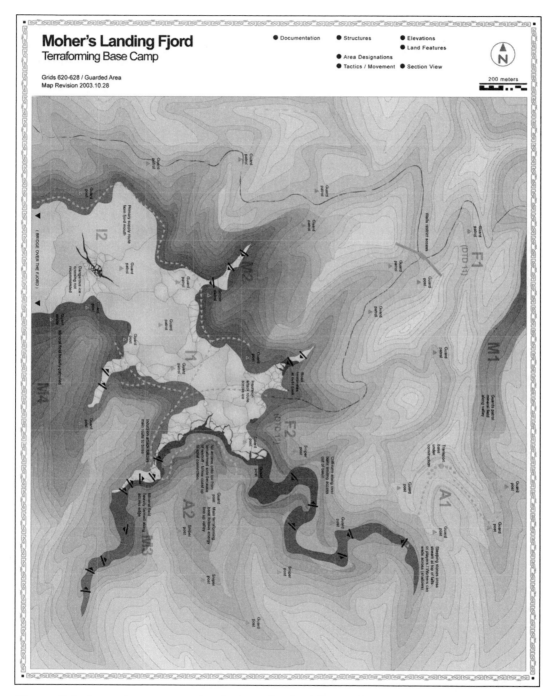

Figure 2.1 A sample game map showing a peninsula with several encounters around a central lake region. This map was generated in Adobe Illustrator by my friend Prem Krishnan.

Next: Write it down. In *The Tempest*, the wizard Prospero causes a storm that ship-wrecks a boatload of noblemen on Prospero's island. He does this because one of the noblemen, Antonio, the Duke of Milan, is his younger brother who betrayed him and took his dukedom, causing him to be exiled on the island. When Prospero arrived there, he fought and defeated an old witch, Sycorax, freeing a magical sprite named Ariel and enslaving the witch's son, Caliban, the beast man.

My game won't need any of the supporting cast, like Miranda, Prospero's daughter, or Sebastian, the King's son. I only need enemies to overcome, so I'll just use Prospero, Ariel, and Caliban. Although none of these characters were evil in the play, my game will be set in an alternate universe where they are. Mua-ha-ha-ha!

Okay, so I have some characters and the basics of a setting. Now I need to come up with some obstacles the player will have to overcome to get to the climactic battle with Prospero himself.

In the play, Prospero summons a ghostly banquet. Ghosts are nice, but I want some-thing with a little more kick. I reach into my game designer bag o' clichés and pull out… zombies! Legions of these things make great obstacles for FPS players. They're already dead, so there's no guilt in blowing their heads off with a shotgun!

Finally, we need some environment obstacles. Caliban lives in a cave, so we might want a cavern of some sort. Shakespeare also includes briar patches and bogs, which will be good for creating mazes.

This is a pretty good start! Now let's list out what we need to create this level.

An island, with islandish stuff:

- Trees
- Bushes
- Sand
- Rocks
- Cliffs
- Briar patches
- Bogs

Wildlife:

- Birds
- Boars (for that *Lord of the Flies* touch, as long as I'm being literary)

Character models:
- A Prospero model
- An Ariel model
- A Caliban model
- Zombie models
- A player model

Object models:
- Weapons!

Architecture models:
- Prospero's house
- Caliban's cave

That seems to be everything I'll need. There's probably more, but this is good for the purposes of this chapter.

Next, I'll draw (very badly) a comic strip illustrating the flow of the level (see Figures 2.2 and 2.3). This will give me a basic idea of how the level will play. It's also fun.

Based on this comic strip, I can see some problems popping up already. For one thing, this level is *huge*! I need a beach, a forest, a cavern complex, a swamp maze, and a huge castle. All this work will take a year and would probably fill four levels, not just one. Conclusion: Get out the scissors, because it's cutting time.

The paper design phase, also called *preproduction*, is the place I want to do my cutting. By identifying problems and obstacles early, I can avoid paying for things I won't use, like art assets or software features. If I'm going to lead a team of artists and designers to create this level and I don't do my cutting until the very end, a lot of work will have been wasted, things that could have been better polished won't be, and I'll have paid the team a lot of money for doing basically nothing.

Since I have five areas, I decide to lose two of them. Looking at the complexity of these areas, the cavern and the swamp seem to be the most intricate. Losing those two areas and moving Caliban and Ariel into the main house seems to make the most sense. So now I'm down to just the beach, the forest surrounding the beach, and Prospero's fortress.

Next I'll create an overhead map of the level, detailing where the different areas and encounters are located (shown in Figure 2.4).

Figure 2.2 Page One of my stunning Masterpiece. And to think people tell me my art hasn't grown since third grade.

Prospero's castle is at the opposite end of the island from where the player starts. That way, the player gets the most out of the level. He also has a good idea which way to go, since the way to the castle is the only path that isn't blocked by the ocean.

For a surprise, I'll stick the castle in a dormant volcano. That way, the player won't know what's coming until he gets to the entrance. I'll place zombies and boars in the little forest to get the player used to some action, and then have the big climax in the volcano.

Since this is turning out to be a fairly small level, we should think about how fast the player will stomp through it, given the weapons I'm giving him (illustrated in the comic strip). Maybe we should provide fewer weapons so that each combat is a tough fight, rather than a *Quake*-esque bloodbath? I'll leave that decision for Chapter 6, when we begin to place our enemies and see how difficult we want to make our combat.

Figure 2.3 Page Two of my epic graphic novel. I'm expecting that you'll see this in a nice, hardbound volume sometime soon in finer comic shops everywhere.

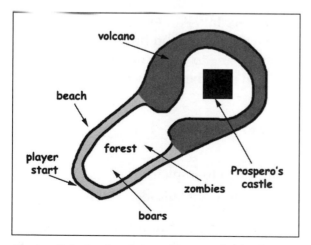

Figure 2.4 Overhead view of Prospero's Island.

What You Have Learned

In this chapter, you learned the following:

- How to come up with great ideas.
- How to test those ideas to make sure they aren't vapor.
- How to write a preliminary design document.
- How to create a functional map.

Now that the paper design is done, we can move to the first step: creating the terrain!

Review Questions

(Answers in Appendix C)

1. Why should you bother to put your game idea on paper, instead of going right to the level editor and cranking it out?
2. How do I come up with great ideas?
3. What is a storyboard?
4. What is a topographical map?

On Your Own

1. Get a dictionary and choose 6 words at random. Out of these six words, choose three and link them together to form the core of an original game idea. For example, let's say my six words are Ink, Fur, Ape, Birdbath, Bread, and Hippopotamus. I choose Hippopotamus, Ape, and Bread. My original game idea: The apes and the hippos are trying to gather as much bread as they can. The player also wants bread and must beat the two animal factions to the carbohydrate-rich delicacy.

2. Using any game idea you'd like, do the following:
   a. Write down the idea.
   b. Choose an appropriate toolset with which to implement it.
   c. Write down any assets you might need to make this idea a reality.

3. Draw a comic strip illustrating the gameplay flow of your level or game. Make sure to have fun with it.

4. Create a map showing the basic landmarks and encounters you'll be adding to your game.

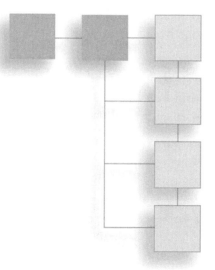

CHAPTER 3

BUILDING
TERRAIN

Terrain is the plate upon which we serve the gourmet dinner of our level. Ha! Is that a corny statement or what? (Get it? *Gourmet? Corn?*)

Corny or not, it's true. If any part of your level takes place in the outdoors, you're going to need terrain. And bad terrain will draw sarcastic and unkind comments from players (to put it gently). So, you need to put a lot of effort into your terrain if you're going to do it right. In fact, most of the effort a professional game developer puts into a game is directed toward making the terrain as beautiful and realistic as possible.

In this chapter, you'll learn:

- The different methods you can use to make terrain
- Some tips on how to make realistic terrain
- Using terrain to serve your gameplay
- Texturing terrain
- Placing props on terrain to flesh out your world

The Importance of Terrain

Along with better looking characters and great special effects, terrain in games continues to grow more and more beautiful as time goes on.

Take a look at the way water has been depicted in games over the past five years. It's gone from a flat blue plane, to an undulating plane with noticeable edges, to a surface that's often more beautiful than the real thing. Terrain is a very, very important part of any level. People walk over terrain on a regular basis. We know what grass, trees, and weeds are supposed to look like. We know that canyon walls are rarely smooth, rocks litter the land, we leave footprints in dirt, and water and wind and gravity mix together to make a chaotic mess everywhere.

Game spaces are rarely chaotic. It's their strength and their weakness. Modeled terrain, at its simplest, is all about smooth planes and nicely rounded corners. It's what terrain would be like if a fanatical cleaning lady were given the powers of a god. In other words, it's totally unrealistic.

So, part of creating terrain is making it messy and chaotic enough to be believable. However, this comes with one glaring problem. Messiness means lots and lots of triangles, the basic building blocks of all 3D computer-generated objects. And the more triangles the computer processor needs to draw, the slower the game gets. Too many triangles, and the computer freezes and crashes.

Terrain, and in fact all 3D modeling for games, is a balancing act between realism and a smooth-running game. The good news is that computers get faster every year. The bad news is that they can't run 100% realistic terrain in real time yet.

So, as a level designer, you always have to pay attention to this balancing act.

Making Terrain

Currently, game toolsets have several ways to make terrain. Each method has strengths and weaknesses that can make your tasks as easy as snapping your fingers, or as hard as untying the Gordian Knot. Nothing is more time-consuming than making a square mile of terrain, and the wrong set of tools can make you feel like you're actually taking a shovel (not the big kind, either, but the plastic kind you make sand castles with at the beach) and moving the dirt yourself.

Heightmaps

A heightmap is a simple 2D picture generated in black, white, and the 254 shades of gray in-between (see Figure 3.1). Mapmakers and geologists use satellite-generated heightmaps to create 3D maps of terrain. The way it works is that each gradient of gray represents a different height. The lighter the color, the higher the terrain. Each gradation of color works out to a height difference in meters, which is variable according to the program that took the picture.

Generating terrain from heightmaps is pretty simple, and it can result in some of the most realistic terrain ever seen in games (see Figure 3.2). It can also mean some of the ugliest terrain, depending upon the game engine and the expertise of the mapmaker. Terrain that's been derived from heightmaps can look angular and rugged, or very smooth and rolling. Blending those two types of terrains can be a nightmare, however.

Creating heightmaps is usually done in one of two ways: 1) Take an existing heightmap from a satellite photo and apply it to your game. This results in terrain that resembles some part of the Earth or one of its close neighbors. 2) Create the map in an image editor, like Photoshop. This takes longer, but it's pretty fun.

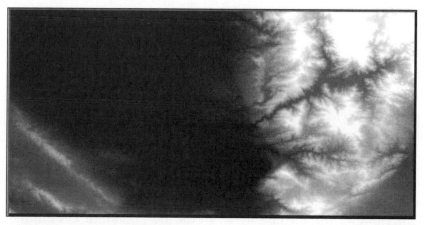

Figure 3.1 A USGS heightmap.

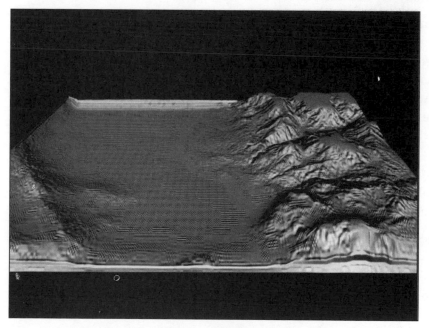

Figure 3.2 Terrain made from the heightmap in Figure 3.1.

Strengths of heightmaps:

- Easy to create
- Easy to make large changes quickly
- Fast iteration time
- Realistic

Weaknesses:

- Hard to make minor changes
- Can take a lot of time to get right
- Resulting terrain tends to look like all other heightmap-generated terrain

Handmade

The next method of generating terrain is to model it by hand. This is obviously very time-consuming work. 3D modelers spend months working on a half-acre of virtual land to get it just right. However, this method allows for the most beautiful, customized terrain you can get. Alien worlds, magical kingdoms, and surreal landscapes can be made so realistic that they take the player's breath away.

Handmade terrain is usually created in a 3D modeling program, like Discreet's 3D Studio Max or Alias Wavefront's Maya. An artist makes a big flat mesh and uses sculpting tools to warp the plane into rough hills and valleys. Then, he touches up various areas, paying closer and closer attention to smaller and smaller details until he's happy with the results. At this point, the lead programmer comes by and faints from seeing all the triangles the artist has used to make the terrain. So, the artist has to start choosing what to cut out, what to simplify, and what to keep. Then the cycle starts again.

Strengths of modeling terrain by hand:

- Finest level of detail possible
- Greatest level of customization
- Small changes are easy to make
- The results are beyond realistic

Weaknesses of modeling terrain by hand:

- Hard to make big changes
- Takes a lot of time
- Can hurt the framerate of the game if the artist isn't careful

Mixed

Because of the weaknesses of both types of terrain editing, game companies sometimes make their own terrain-editing tools that try to combine the heightmap's ease of making large areas of terrain with the fine control of the hand-modeling packages. These tools can sometimes be hard to work with, and they don't tend to be as strong or as easy to use as tools that do one or the other.

The major 3D packages, Maya and 3D Studio Max, allow for the importing of heightmaps, and with some effort, they can give you the control to make very fine adjustments. These are expensive, complex tools, though, and it may be hard for the normal mod-builder to afford a version that actually gives them the functionality they need. There are less-expensive modeling programs available, but, with less expense may come less versatility. I advise you to experiment as much as you can with as many packages as you can to see which one works the best for you.

Strengths of mixed-terrain tools:

- Combine the strengths of the two fundamental tools

Weaknesses:

- Expensive
- Usually aren't as strong as a tool that's used for one specific method
- Complex to use

Autogenerated

Next, there are programs that automatically generate terrain (see Figure 3.3). Autogenerated terrain is useful when the player doesn't need to interact with the terrain very much, except to know where it is. Flight simulators sometimes use autogenerated terrain if the player is usually spending most of his time above the clouds.

Strength of autogenerated terrain tools:

- You don't need to worry about terrain

Weakness of autogenerated terrain tools:

- Very little customization ability

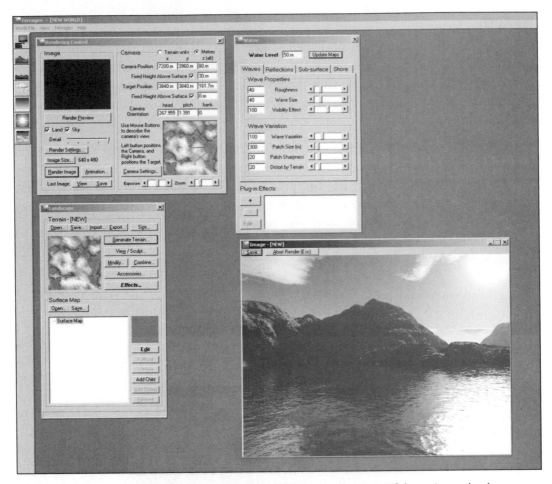

Figure 3.3 The Terragen program by Planetside Software creates beautiful terrain randomly.

Tiled Terrain

Many third-person games, including real-time strategy games such as *Age of Empires* and roleplaying games like *Neverwinter Nights*, use tiles to make their terrain (see Figure 3.4). Tiles are pregenerated squares of land that can be placed next to each other to make an infinite variety of landscapes.

Using tiles is pretty easy. The designer picks a tile, drags it to the place he wants, and goes back for more. Some games allow you to modify the tiles, changing textures and landscape types to make deserts or grasslands or forests. Tiles are a great way to make terrain when the player isn't going to be looking extremely closely at the ground, but they're not intended for terrain with great variations in altitude.

Strengths of tileset terrain creation:

- Very easy and fun to use
- Quick creation time

Weaknesses of tileset terrain creation:

- Limited to the tiles and terrain objects that come with the tileset
- Usually only used for games that use an overhead isometric camera view
- Not very good at making big altitude changes

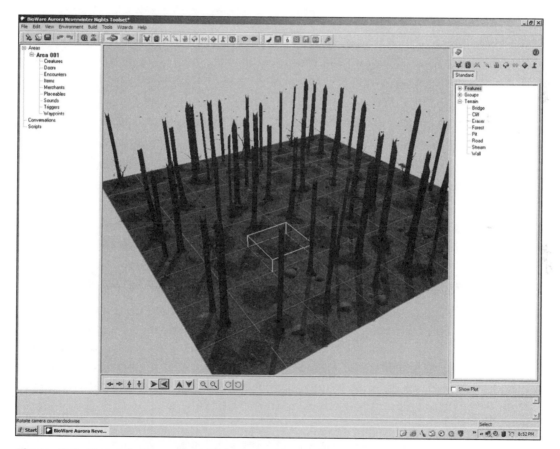

Figure 3.4 Bioware's *Neverwinter Nights* Aurora Design Tool, showing a piece of tiled terrain.

Terrain and Gameplay

Making terrain can be extremely fun. It's a creative task that becomes a sort of micro-management strategy game after a while, as you nudge and tweak to get things just right. Because of this, it's very easy to forget that terrain serves one purpose: *to make the game more fun.* In your effort to create a beautiful landscape, you may unintentionally create weaknesses in your game. Players may find themselves lost or frustrated, or even worse, they may find loopholes in your level and exploit them to cheat. To avoid this, always keep in mind what the core gameplay is in your level, and that you need to create the terrain to suit that gameplay.

Some hints for making terrain:

- Make only as much terrain as you need. Don't create spaces that you'll fill with Easter Eggs "later." Believe me, those spaces will present themselves without overplanning on your part. Furthermore, making huge spaces means lots of running for the player, and that means lots of work for you.
- Mazes aren't fun in and of themselves, unless that's the point of the game.
- Hidden paths are frustrating. Use them sparingly.
- Don't make paths that fail to reward the player. If a player follows a path, it should lead to somewhere important or something fun to do.
- Always be consistent. If a certain incline is impassable in one place, that angle of hillside should be impassable everywhere else. If a certain denseness of forest is impassable in one place, an equal denseness shouldn't be passable somewhere else.

Another Purpose for Terrain: Fencing the Player In

So far, we've talked about terrain as something the player walks on. However, terrain can serve a second purpose: defining the limits of the area the player can explore. Many times, a level designer will place his outdoor level within a canyon or valley, where unassailable hillsides and cliffs keep the player from going beyond the borders of the level. Other times, an unswimmable ocean or a clearly marked wasteland, such as a desert, give the player visual clues as to where he can't go.

When you're making the "fence" around your level, remember these tips:

- Always clearly mark the areas where the player can't go. Your fences will be frustrating to the player, as a rule. No one likes being forbidden from going where they want to go. However, if you make the fence clearly recognizable, the player will understand that they're part of the game, not just the whim of the game designer to forbid exploration. Even an invisible wall preventing a player from going into a barren desert can be forgiven if the line is clearly marked.

- Don't put anything interesting on the other side of the fence, unless it's obviously unattainable, such as something too far away to walk to, like a floating palace or far off mountain range. Nothing is worse than seeing someplace you want to explore and finding your way blocked. Putting a building or a statue or a cave opening on the other side of your fence will make the player think he's supposed to go exploring. He'll waste a lot of time trying to get over there, and he won't be happy when he realizes it's impossible. Just because you don't think it's significant doesn't mean the player won't.

Impassability Regions

Sometimes you'll want to put a barrier in front of the player to make sure he doesn't wander off the side of your world or walk somewhere you don't want him to go. In most game engines, you can create an impassability region, an area that stops the player from progressing any further.

Impassability regions are usually invisible, and the player can get frustrated walking into them. Therefore, you should put a lot of thought into where you place these regions. Make sure that the player understands why he's being prevented from going where he wants to go. He needs to *see* why he's being restricted, so put up a fence, create a wall, change the ground color, make the forest denser, or do something just as obvious.

Some game engines allow the player to walk up any angle less than 90 degrees. You'll probably have to lay down impassability regions on all slopes that will be too steep for the player to climb. Always make sure you're consistent about which angles the player can and can't climb up. He may notice even a little variation, and it'll upset his sense of continuity.

This also goes for types of terrain that you're making impassable due to the supposed danger of walking on them, like lava or mucky swampland. Make absolutely sure that the terrain is textured in such a way that the passable areas are easily distinguishable from the impassable areas.

Making Realistic Terrain

Nature is chaotic. It's not made of organized lines and perfect curves. However, there's a balancing act between drawing all those triangles and keeping the game playable, and chaos takes a lot of time to create with a tool that uses straight lines and perfect curves as building blocks. So, you have to concentrate your more detailed scenery in places where the player is likely to go. For instance, if the player is confined to walking along the bottom of a canyon, it's best to make everything detailed from the ground up to just above eye-level, and then simplify from there as you go up the wall.

Also, make sure you have good source material. It really helps to have a few good pictures of the type of terrain you're trying to create, so you can make it as realistic as possible. *National Geographic* and travel books are prime sources of good terrain photos.

Here are some tips on specific terrain types.

Mountains:

There are very few game engines that can make mountains truly mountainous. Most real mountains cover miles and miles of surface area, most of it vertical, which would strain the limits of any game engine. However, mountainsides are pretty popular in games, especially as fence walls. Another good thing about mountains is that they can look jagged and angular, which game engines do really well. One thing to remember, however, is that it's usually not very fun to fight on hillsides, especially in close-combat games where the player is fighting hand-to-hand. Make sure you have some flatter spots for those encounters.

Hills:

Game engines also do hills and other rolling landscapes pretty well. If done right, hills are good for obscuring encounters until the player runs right into the other character(s). However, hills can obscure landmarks as well, so make sure that your terrain is set up so that the player can get reoriented if he finds himself lost.

Desert, plains, arctic wastes, and other flatlands:

Flatlands are rarely flat. They have slight hills and valleys, and they can be home to rivers and ravines. Even the most boring terrain has some chaos in it. Try to mix things up with slight altitude deviations, strategically placed plants (where appropriate), and maybe a hill or two to provide landmarks.

Rivers and lakes:

If the game engine you're using allows the player to swim, they'll want to go into any water you put in front of them. Always make sure the player can get out of anything he gets into, especially rivers and lakes. Don't make the banks so steep that a player who jumps into the river to see if there are any ammo crates at the bottom can't get back out.

If your game engine doesn't allow swimming, make sure you set up impassability regions in front of all bodies of water. This will maintain the illusion that the players *could* swim if they really wanted to. Once again, don't put anything interesting on the other side of the water unless you have a way for the player to get over there.

Pits, canyons, and ravines:

If the player falls into a crevice or a pit, there should be a way for him to get out. Even if you think that the fall itself will mean certain death, provide some sort of one-way secret path or teleport pad. That way, the sneaky player who manages to figure out how to get down there without going squish can get back up to the top.

Canyons and ravines are a great way to funnel the player to a place you want him to go. That's why they're in just about every game. Try to think of ways to avoid overusing this terrain type, so you won't be caught in the same trap so many other level designers have fallen into before.

Making Terrain Fun

Entertaining the player is the primary duty of the game maker, of course. Everything you do as you're making the game should aim toward that target, including creating terrain.

Establish mood:

Terrain is used primarily to establish atmosphere. At its best, it immerses the player into the world, making him feel like he's actually climbing through mountain trails or hacking through dank jungles. To accomplish this, you should make your terrain as realistic as possible given the limits of your game engine, and it should be appropriate to the characters the player meets. For instance, a player probably shouldn't be meeting a penguin in the desert. (Unless the penguin has sunglasses on.)

Terrain can build tension:

Terrain can be used to build tension in the game by hiding upcoming encounters, or by being dangerous in and of itself. Some rocky terrain or a dense copse of trees can hide lurking foes, or maybe a small chest containing a valuable resource. A lava pool or steep precipice can add a sense of peril, requiring the player to watch where he's going as he's also looking out for nearby menaces. Tension can also be built as the player uses that same terrain to hide from the eyes of passing enemies.

Terrain can relieve tension:

A quiet pool hidden in the bushes or a peaceful ruin can provide a relaxing moment after a long-running battle. Try to make your terrain's tension level ebb and flow from tense to relaxed. This makes for a better gameplay experience than all-tense-all-the-time.

Terrain can tell story:

A carving on a rock face, a crop circle, a perfect line of trees, a ditch, a trail, a road, and a set of tracks in the snow all tell stories. One of my favorite moments playing *Dark Age of Camelot* was when a friend and I got to the top of a hill and noticed a huge drawing of a bull etched into another nearby hill. I was asking, "Who made that? What does it mean?"

Terrain can be fun to run or drive over:

In a game where you can drive vehicles, you should provide a few non-lethal bumps to give the player some air under his wheels. A row of stones can be a fun little jumping puzzle for the player who just wants to move around. Terrain that's broken and hard to traverse can spoil the player's fun, though, especially if there's a lot of it.

Terrain can be beautiful:

Terrain can fill the player with awe and wonder. Beautiful terrain enhances the fun of any game. Besides being beautiful, terrain can also be creepy, boring, or whatever you need to reinforce the mood of your level.

Terrain and Strategy

The famous Chinese strategist and general Sun Tzu wrote, "The natural formation of the country is the soldier's best ally." Military scholars throughout the ages have studied the tactical advantages and disadvantages inherent in different types of terrain.

If you're creating combat levels, you need to remember the tactical aspects of your terrain as well as the aesthetic ones. As technology progresses and computers can do more and more calculations per second, game physics are approaching lifelike levels. With this comes gravitational and atmospheric influences on projectiles, increased difficulty running up hills and increased ease running down them, and lifelike systems where one game object can affect another. All this means that tactical lessons regarding terrain and environment developed throughout history will become increasingly useful in gaming environments.

The height advantage:

This is a pretty basic advantage you can have over a foe. Being up on a hill means your arrows and bullets go farther, and your enemy has a harder time rushing your position. It's also easier for your troops to retreat, as long as there's a way off the hill that isn't straight into the enemy. However, since good hills are usually rare, a hilltop can expose your existence to the enemy much sooner than being hidden in a valley does. And if your army is too small, your forces can be surrounded easily.

The access advantage:

An area like a canyon or a hard-to-access valley can work to your advantage, restricting access to your position so your foe can't approach with all his forces at once. However, usually this means that you can't retreat very easily. Once again, this type of terrain advantage means you're restricting your troops to a confined area, where they might become surrounded.

The advantage of flat terrain:

Flat terrain allows for maximum ease of movement and deployment of forces. This is good for cavalry and vehicles because they can react in battle more dynamically.

The dangers of terrain:

Many types of terrain are dangerous or hinder troop movement. Swamps and loose sand can slow your troops down considerably, as can ice and heavily forested areas.

Players will recognize strategically potent areas and use them to their advantage. Be one step ahead of them and create terrain that puts them in interesting tactical situations, like dealing with a small band of foes shooting arrows from a cliffside, or fighting through a series of small, interconnected islands in an otherwise impenetrable swamp. Give the player the chance to come up with his own solutions, and you'll be regarded as a genius in the field.

Texturing Terrain

As I've mentioned, terrain is greatly improved by the addition of appropriate *textures*, or images that are placed on the surfaces of 3D objects. A texture can be as simple as a color or as complex as a human face. In professional game making, artists are hired to work exclusively on textures. Believe me, a good texture artist is worth his or her weight in gold.

When you're making terrain, you'll need to texture it after it's done. Each engine and 3D toolset has its own way of applying textures to a 3D surface, but there are some general things you can think about that will help.

- As always, only choose textures that are appropriate for the setting. Green textures over your desert or arctic level will make it look like rolling hills in the spring.
- Make sure your textures tile well. When you have a repeating texture, it has a seam between each segment unless the texture's edges blend well. This is why those texture artists are so valuable. Making seamless textures is very difficult.

- Dark textures should be used sparingly. Most moving objects, which are usually pretty dark themselves, will disappear against dark textures. Players who can't see their foes get frustrated easily. If you want things to be dark, use dim lighting rather than dark textures.

- Keep it simple. Terrain is meant to enhance the level, not overwhelm it. Saturating your level with bright, clashing colors and reflective surfaces might cause some players to avoid your work in the future. Also, reflective surfaces like glass or metal require extra processing power that might be better used somewhere else, such as allowing your player to move more than one step every few seconds.

Terrain Props

After you've built and textured your terrain, you'll want to start landscaping it with objects like trees, grass, bushes, rocks, small buildings, walls, and whatever else you feel is necessary. However, you'll have to carefully plan what objects you use and how you place them in order to maximize their effect on the player.

Placing Objects on Your Terrain

As always, when you're placing any object or item in your game, you'll have to consider its effect on the game's speed. In years past, most things like trees and bushes were either too expensive in terms of processor consumption to render or too ugly when they were cheap, so many games didn't bother with them unless absolutely necessary. But now processor speed has increased enough that you can put a lot of props in a level without endangering the framerate too much. There are also many tricks for making these things even cheaper.

One of the limitations of game engines is that they can't handle a huge variety of different objects at the same time. That's because the engine needs to load each object into memory before it can render it. However, multiple copies, or *instances*, of an object are cheaper, since the program only has to load the object once and then can use that information again and again for every copy. Unfortunately, this can make a level seem very artificial. After all, in real life you never see two trees that look *exactly* alike. However, there are some tricks you can use to alleviate this problem slightly.

- Don't put things that look exactly alike right next to each other at exactly the same angle. Having two boulders sitting together that look exactly alike is very noticeable. The exceptions to this are manmade objects, like columns or walls, which players won't think twice about.

- Second, if you have to put two copies of an object next to one another, it helps to rotate one of them so that the player is seeing two different views of it. This works better if the objects are fairly complex, like trees.

- Try not to create copies of groups of objects. If you have a clump of four trees, and then another clump of four trees that looks exactly like it just down the road, your level begins to look very fake.

Another way game makers build terrain objects cheaply is to generate them automatically. Usually, these are small, often-repeated objects with no collision, like grass, small bushes, or weeds. Sometimes, this is done with larger objects as well, like trees and rocks. To implement this, you create an area on your terrain map that tells the game engine to place a bunch of copies of a certain object randomly. This type of prop generation is very efficient and is used a lot in newer engines. However, because it uses repeated objects, sometimes it can lead to the aforementioned problems.

Tip

One of the things that really slows down processor speed is collision. When an object has collision, it means the player can't walk through it, like a wall or a tree. The game engine needs to monitor it constantly to see if anything has run into it. Some terrain props that the player doesn't expect to impede his progress, like grass and weeds and bushes, don't need collision, so you can use more of that type of object. Trees and rocks need to have collision, on the other hand, so they're more expensive to use.

Gameplay Effects of Terrain Props

Here are some things to consider when you're placing objects on your terrain.

As always, only use objects that make sense for the setting. Palm trees don't belong on the tundra, and huge ice stalagmites don't belong on tropical islands.

Don't let your landscaping interfere with the eyeline of the player, especially in "hot zones" where the player is likely to be in combat. It might be appealing to design a running battle between trees, like in the movies *Ninja Scroll* and *Crouching Tiger, Hidden Dragon*, but it's frustrating for the player if he can't immediately find who's shooting him and shoot back. It's also frustrating when the player can't see any objects on the ground that he wants to pick up, or a foe's body that he can loot.

Terrain props can be used as landmarks. A repeated item, like distinctively shaped stones or dead trees, can help the player identify the path that you want him to go down. Be careful with this, however, and only use landmark objects as landmark objects. A randomly placed marker stone can confuse or mislead your player, and he probably won't trust your use of landmarks again.

Terrain props should be considered the lowest-priority items in your level. If your level is running slow, and you can't reduce the size of the level terrain at all, these are the objects you should cut first.

Example: The Building of Prospero's Island

To illustrate the task of terrain building, I'm going to build Prospero's Island, the level I designed on paper in the last chapter. I chose Crytek's Sandbox level editor to do this, because 1) It's specifically designed for creating islands, 2) It ships with *Far Cry*, which is a very pretty game, and 3) It's actually pretty slick. Many times, the level editor that ships with a game can be pretty buggy and difficult to work with. While the Sandbox has its issues, it suits my needs and works pretty well.

The first step is to create the terrain itself. The Sandbox uses heightmaps to start with, and then I can do finer edits within the level display itself. Because the heightmap creation tool is a bit clumsy, I decided to make a first pass in Photoshop instead, and then import the heightmap into the game (see Figure 3.5).

There's a low beach area that leads into something that looks like a dead volcano. I decide to make the level very small, with room for only a few encounters, since it's only for demonstration purposes.

I then import the map into the Sandbox program (see Figure 3.6).

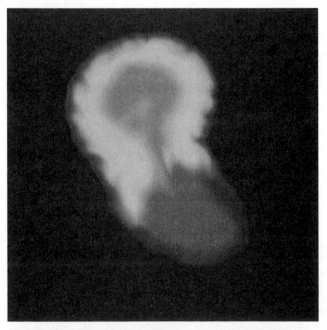

Figure 3.5 The initial heightmap.

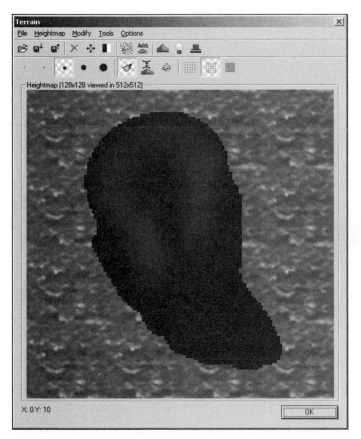

Figure 3.6 The heightmap transformed!

This is then rendered into the level editor, after some fine tweaking to get rid of some ridges (see Figure 3.7).

Now the terrain is done. It's time to do a texture pass. I decide to stick to the basics: a rock texture, a grass texture, and a sand texture for the beach. The Sandbox editor has a terrain-texturing tool (shown in Figure 3.8), which is very nice to use. It allows you to place textures by height, which means you can have sand textures from 0-16 meters into the air, grass from 16-17 meters, and rock the rest of the way up.

Once again, this process isn't perfect, and I need to do some tweaking and painting within the editor itself to get my desired effect. After generating all the textures, my lump of rock looks more like an actual island (see Figure 3.9).

Figure 3.7 The basic form of the island.

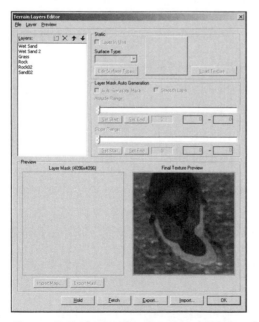

Figure 3.8 The Sandbox terrain texturing tool. This is by far the best texturing tool I've used for terrain.

Figure 3.9 The island begins to look more like a real place with textures on it.

With the texturing done, it's time to add terrain props. Right now, the player has a clear shot at the volcano, where I'm going to put Prospero's house. I want the path to be somewhat indirect, so he can't make a beeline straight there, and I want to place some zombie and pig encounters. I decide to place some large rocks on the island to create some twists and turns (see Figure 3.10).

The player now has several paths from his starting point on the beach.

Next, I need to place some plants to further bring the island to life. Placing plants is fairly easy in the Sandbox editor (see Figures 3.11 and 3.12). You can place them one at a time, or use a brush-like tool to lay down bulk plants. I won't lie to you, it takes a while to experiment with the plant objects that come with the editor, and to place the objects you want without making them look too much like clones.

Figure 3.10 Volcanic rocks create narrow passages that create choices for the player.

Figure 3.11 Adding plants makes for a more realistic experience and obscures the player's view, increasing the feeling of mystery and danger.

Figure 3.12 Adding an interior forest to the island. There are well over a thousand plants in this view!

Now the island finally looks decent enough to start on the next step: Prospero's Mansion!

What You Have Learned

In this chapter, you learned the following:

- The different ways to create terrain: heightmap, modeled, autogenerated, mixed, and tile.
- How terrain can affect gameplay.
- How to start making your terrain fun and tactically challenging.
- How to texture your terrain.
- How to place static, decorative objects on your terrain, like plants or rocks.

In the next chapter, you'll learn how to create and place buildings and their interiors. Finally, something to put on all this terrain we've been talking about!

Review Questions

(Answers in Appendix C)

1. How does a heightmap work?
2. What's frustrating to a player?
   a) Invisible walls
   b) A lack of landmarks
   c) Not being able to see his opponent
   d) All of the above

3. Name three ways that terrain can be fun.
4. What are some of the things you have to consider when texturing your terrain?
5. What are some of the things you have to consider when placing props on your terrain?

On Your Own

For this chapter's exercise, choose an editor and create some terrain. I'd like you to make two different maps:

1. The first map: Make the worst possible terrain you can. Experiment with your editor, and try to do everything wrong: spiky hills, blind alleys, everything textured pink and green, etc. Try to make it as ugly and implausible as you possibly can. If you're in a class, set up a judging panel and give out prizes for the most insane map. Have fun with this. This will be your "learning map," where you get to push all the buttons in your chosen editor and see what they all do.

2. The second map: Take the lessons you've learned from the ugly map about how to create terrain, and build the map you designed on paper in the previous chapter. Don't hesitate to make it much smaller than you had planned. Although you don't want a cramped map, you need to refrain from making something so large that you'll never have enough time to create it or enough bandwidth to run it. If you can easily drop the map into the game and run around in it, try not to make it bigger than what your character can run in 30-45 seconds from end to end.

CHAPTER 4

BUILDING ARCHITECTURE AND SPACES

Many games rely solely on designer-created architecture to be the environment for their games. From true-to-scale buildings found in real life to strange alien structures, game designers have used just about everything you can imagine as settings for their games.

As a level designer, it will be your job to create these environments and place them within your game. This task can be one of the most time-consuming jobs in level design, and your ability to create fun, interesting places for the player to explore will often determine whether your game wins their adulation or their sneering derision.

In this chapter, you'll learn the following:

- How to create architecture and spaces using various toolsets
- How to design your environment by making architecture that fits within your game world
- How to make architecture that's fun and supports your gameplay
- How to texture your architecture

Creating Architecture and Spaces Using Toolsets

There are about as many ways to make structures in games as there are toolsets. However, most of those toolsets work in similar ways, which means that we can separate how to build architecture into a few easy-to-understand subgroups.

Brushes

The first time I noticed the word "brush" in relation to level creation was when I started experimenting with making levels for the game *Quake*. It confused me completely. Ordinarily, I would think of a brush as something you use to paint a portrait. However, in level editors, a brush is a form that you use to make simple or complex 3D objects within your game world. It's kind of like a three-dimensional stencil.

In editors like UnrealEd for Epic's *Unreal* engine, brushes are both additive and subtractive. The level designer can create objects, like a big square or sphere, or even a custom-made shape. They can also take bites out of existing objects, such as making a rectangular hole in a wall to make a doorway. Some editors require that you use a huge brush to make the initial space you will be working in, by subtracting a shape out of nothing, which can be a hard notion to get your head around. With some creativity, you can combine adding and subtracting shapes to make very complex architecture and environments.

The term "brush" can also be used for imported objects that you copy again and again within your level, like a tree or small house. *Far Cry's* Sandbox, which we've been using for our examples, uses this terminology.

Many level editors for first-person shooters use this type of architectural creation. It can sometimes be a steep learning curve to create spaces in this way, but once you understand the basics, it's pretty simple. With only minutes of work, you can be running around in your own personalized level. (Of course, you might be confined to what amounts to a big box, but what do you expect to whip up in only a few minutes?)

3D Modeling Software

Another way to make architecture is to use a professional 3D modeling software package like Alias' Maya package, Discreet's 3DS MAX, or Newtek's Lightwave. These programs are much more powerful than your standard level editor, and you can use them to create just about anything you want in terms of architecture. Most professional game studios use these programs to generate their buildings and environments. However, they're expensive, and you need some sort of exporting software to place the models you make into your game.

In my experience, this can be very difficult and frustrating. Many of these exporting programs are unsupported and buggy, and game engines are very picky about what you can and cannot import. However, sometimes having the power and stability of a professional 3D package can really make up for the pain, when your only other recourse is to use an unstable or dysfunctional level editor that comes with the game.

Tilesets

One more way to generate architecture is through the tilesets that come with the game's level editor. Some games, like Bioware's *Neverwinter Nights*, use Lego-like modular tilesets that allow you to snap together walls and the like to create a building (see Figure 4.1). Other level editors come with entire prebuilt rooms or buildings that you can connect to make bigger structures. This is undoubtedly the easiest way to whip up a level. However, you have much less freedom to make unique-looking buildings, since you get only a few modules to work with.

Figure 4.1 A castle being assembled in the *Neverwinter Nights* toolset.

Designing Your Environment

You probably have an idea about the kinds of buildings you want in your game. They may be part of a re-creation of the local mall, or a super-abstract set of floating platforms for a fast deathmatch map. For both of those structures, and everything in-between, there are some general ideas that you need to keep in mind while creating your dream-scape.

Imagine you're an Olympic-class runner. You can run a mile in just under 4 minutes. Now, imagine that you move around at full speed all the time. No slow walks, no careful movement, just very fast starts and stops. Imagine how hard it would be to move around your house or apartment like that. How hard would it be to navigate between your coffee table and couch at a full sprint to get to the TV? How hard would it be to run full-speed through doors and small entrances, or to browse the clothes racks in your favorite store like somebody's chasing you? It would be difficult.

However, this is what most games are set up to do. Players find it boring to move slowly and always want to get to their destination as fast as possible, so games set up the characters to move at about the pace of an Olympic runner's sprint.

As a level designer, it's imperative that you consider player movement in all your designs. Your furniture must be placed in such a way that players can easily maneuver around it at a full tilt. Your rooms and buildings must be large enough for characters to move through easily, and your roadways and sidewalks must also be designed to take this speed into consideration.

Another aspect of architecture you'll need to account for is size. Normally, the player's sense of scale in a game is somewhat skewed. Everything onscreen seems smaller than it actually is. When built to exact scale, furniture looks like it was made for children, spaces seem too tightly packed, and ceilings look too low.

Does this mean that you'll have to make everything huge when you're designing your level? The answer is no. You just need to be aware of what it will feel like for the player to navigate around your level. This means constantly exporting your level and running around in it to make sure that it feels comfortable, realistic, and fun. Before you put in one enemy, or one puzzle, always launch your game and make sure that it *feels* good to play. I know that's less than scientific, but it's part of the "art" of making games. Keep playing and playing your level, trying out everything from running to one side of the level and then the other to just hanging out in one room and shooting at imaginary enemies. Make sure you can see everything you want the player to see, get to all the places you want your players to go.

Try to keep travel times short. If the player has to spend more than 30 seconds running full-tilt from one action point to another, you might want to consider tightening up your spaces or redesigning your rooms to be a bit smaller.

Architecture

Since the dawn of civilization, mankind has tried to create structures that are both functional and beautiful. From ancient Babylonian cities to the pyramids of Egypt to the modern skyscraper, architects have devoted their talents to creating artistic living spaces.

Today's game makers can create fantastic structures never dreamed of by architects throughout history, due to one simple advantage: We don't have to pay attention to the laws of physics!

We don't have to think of how gravity affects our structures. We don't have to think of load-bearing walls, or how an arch is both beautiful and does a very good job of keeping the wall above it from collapsing. Our mighty bridges won't collapse suddenly due to the harmonics of a stray gust of wind. Our dams can be so thin they're invisible when you look at them from the side, and yet they can hold back oceans of water. We can have upside-down pyramids that stand rock-solid on their tips, mile-high skyscrapers, floating cities, and dungeons buried deep beneath the earth with no supports to keep the tons of rock above them from collapsing.

On the other hand, making structures like this can take away from the reality of a game. If you don't make some sort of nod to how real structures work, players can't immerse themselves in your game. Therefore, always make your structures at least *somewhat* believable. You don't need to put support columns everywhere, or make sure your creations are "up to code," but walls should have thickness, as should floors and counters and furniture. Buildings should at least *look* like they can stand up on their own, and you should always provide a surface that's solid-looking for the player to run on.

Although many of the compromises that architects have to make with the laws of physics can be ignored in virtual landscapes, a lot of the same design principles still hold weight. You don't need to be trained as an architect to be a level designer, but many of the best professionals in the game industry do have formal training in design and architecture. As you continue your education beyond this introductory book, you might consider picking up some elementary architectural design books to see how the real guys approach it.

One of the fundamental aspects of architectural design is how spaces push and pull people. Wide open spaces are inviting to people, drawing them in. Closed spaces and pinched corners push people away, making them feel trapped. By alternating spaces that pull and spaces that push in their structures, architects create a flow that keeps people moving from space to space, looking at the things the architects want them to look at and ignoring the parts that don't add to the aesthetics.

Architects are also masters of using different textures and colors to enhance the flavor of an environment. The different types of building materials, the angles and corners (or no corners at all), the color of the paint, and the sculptures or furniture all work together to create the environment. A large part of the architect's art is creating mood and immersion, and the same goes for game designers. Studying architectural design can be extremely valuable when you want to leap from building simple spaces to constructing works of art.

Inside vs. Outside

One thing you'll always have to consider is that the outside of a structure should always look big enough to contain the inside. In the real world, physics comes into play and the outside of a building actually contains all the stuff that's inside. Whereas in games, going inside a building sometimes means entering a whole new level that isn't actually within the environs of that building. This allows the designer to make the interior as vast as he wants, but it can jar that sense of immersion.

In most cases, I've seen it dealt with like this: When a building leads into a whole new level, the designer makes sure the player can see only a facade of the building or structure he's about to enter. The player might see a door set in a rock wall, for instance, which leads into an immense underground base filled with angry mutant chinchillas.

Immersion

Possibly even more than terrain, architecture is incredibly powerful at communicating your game's mood to the player. Urban, rural, futuristic, post-apocalyptic, medieval, fantastic, or just plain modern-day architecture helps reinforce the *immersion* of your level. Making your architecture as appropriate as possible to your game's theme is instrumental in immersing the player into your world.

Once you've decided on a theme and a setting, it's then your responsibility to be as faithful to that setting as possible. Make sure you research your setting thoroughly to ensure the architecture exudes the atmosphere you want to convey.

Occluders and Portals

Remember the old philosophical question "if a tree falls in the woods, and there's no one there to hear it, does it make a sound?" When designing levels, you need to ask yourself a similar question: "If a player enters a building, do I really need the outside world to continue to exist?"

Everything in your game will require some portion of your computer's processor to create and maintain. Some things take up more of the processor's time than others, but it's always good to figure out ways to take the load off of its back. One good way to do this is to tell the game engine not to draw anything the player can't see.

In the real world, when you enter your house, you lose sight of most of the things outside of it. You might not be able to see your front yard, or inside the garage, or your neighbors down the street. However, those things are still there. Games are much the same: When you enter the dank warehouse, the game continues to draw all the stuff outside the warehouse that you saw on the way in. Unlike the real world, everything outside that warehouse is taking up processor time, and thus slowing your game down. To save on that loss, many game toolsets allow you to set up regions that tell the computer to stop drawing things that the player no longer has the ability to see.

This process is called *portalling*. This term is slightly misleading: When I first heard it, it confused me greatly. What it refers to is the portals that connect one area to another, but the entire process is much deeper.

Occluders

Occluders are objects that hide, or occlude, whatever is beyond them. Occluders can take the shape of a simple plane, or can come in 3D shapes, like boxes. When the player is on one side of an occluder, everything behind that occluder is no longer drawn, saving valuable processor cycles.

Plane-shaped occluders are usually used for very large areas, used to hide entire buildings or large swathes of terrain. A level designer places them in areas where he knows the player won't be able to see anything that would be hidden anyway so that large chunks of his level aren't draining processor power away from what is immediately interesting the player (see Figure 4.2). These can be dangerous, however, if the player manages to squeeze into a space where his view could see whatever the occluder is hiding, as he'll see big empty spaces where architecture and terrain should be.

Box-shaped occluders are used mainly to hide the interiors of buildings from players on the outside. This type of occlusion is used in most types of first- and third-person action games, and is usually required to keep the game's framerate moving along swiftly.

Another note about occluders is that players can walk right through them. While they are barriers to sight, they aren't barriers to the player. If a player walks through an occluder wall, or into an occluded area, whatever was hidden from him will pop into view! This can be pretty disconcerting, and is usually not what you want to happen.

Portals

Many times, you'll want the player to see what is behind an occluder without having to drop the occluder altogether. You'll want the player to see inside a doorway, or through a window. In these cases, you'll want to use a portal.

Portals are the interfaces between occluders and whatever is outside them. Placing a portal on the surface of an occluder allows the player to see what is directly behind that portal, and not much else (see Figure 4.3).

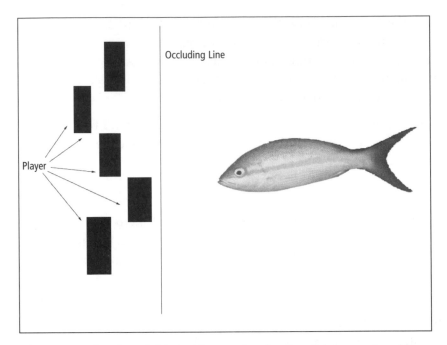

Figure 4.2 The player is blocked from seeing the giant fish by a series of large warehouses. In this case, a level designer can put an occluder behind the buildings so the fish won't be drawn. Once the player gets to a position where he's just about to see the fish, the designer can turn off the occluder so it is revealed in all its aquatic glory moments before the player turns the corner.

You'll want to place portals on every entrance and exit from an occluder box. Place them on each window as well.

Using Portals and Occluders

Portals and occluders are used fairly regularly in complex levels. Though all toolsets are different, there is some common functionality that generally occurs.

In my experience, I've found that giant occluders are rarely used, as they can cause big hiccups in performance when the occluder drops and a large number of objects are suddenly drawn. The cases I've seen where they were seriously considered were in city areas where the performance was low because there were so many buildings being drawn. An occluder would be used to raise performance by keeping large amounts of the city invisible.

When using any type of occluder, you'll usually have to associate all the objects that you want to occlude to it. This is done in many ways, from having to go into an object's properties and identifying the occluder, to just having to have that object

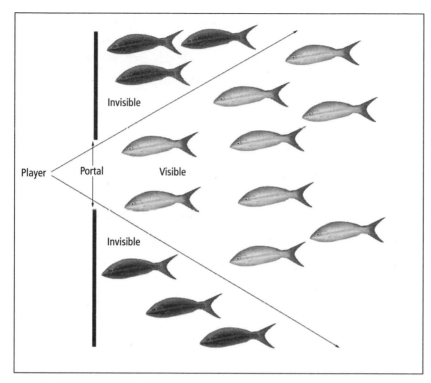

Figure 4.3 The player is looking through a portal into an area swarming with fish. The game engine reveals all the fish within the viewing area of the player, but keeps those fish outside the viewing area hidden.

within that occluder's space. One of the common mistakes with occluders is mis-linking an object; then it will turn invisible at the wrong time. Keep an eye out for this problem because, even though an object is invisible, it often can retain its collision, which means players will bump into stuff they can't see.

Usually, objects can only belong to one occluder at a time. Having an object associated with more than one occluder usually creates problems in some way, from objects that vanish and appear from one moment to another to weird collision problems.

When two occluders are near one another, a few problems can crop up. If you have two rooms, for instance, and each have a different occluder associated with them, the walls between the two occluders become contested areas. In cases like this, you'll usually want your walls to be made from two one-sided pieces, where each occluder has its own set of walls.

Try not to overlap occluders, as this can cause problems, as well.

A portal, in most engines, must be linked to the occluder it's attached to. If it is a portal between two occluded areas, then it has to be linked to both those occluders. Once again, not linking these correctly can cause weird bugs to happen, where you are seeing areas through portals that should be invisible.

Game Architecture Types

Architecture types vary from one game genre to another. It's convenient to use architectural clichés to immerse the player into the game more quickly. This may not settle well with your artistic sense. But if a player has to deal with an unexpected or unknown style of architecture, he'll spend as much time trying to figure out where he is as he does enjoying your gameplay. In essence, this makes your game half as fun.

Always remember, your audience won't go through the same creative process you do when you're designing your level. You might spend several hours designing an environment that combines a society of crawfish-worshipping Creole bricklayers with the technology of *Blade Runner* and the architectural sense of the ancient Sumerians, but most players will just walk through your Crab City and be confused.

The following are some basic stylistic guidelines for the more widely used architectural clichés in today's games.

Fantasy

In games, the fantasy genre is where you find dragons and wizards and such, usually in a medieval setting. Fantasy architecture varies quite a bit. There's always a big difference between the architecture of the good guys and the bad guys. The good guys have lots of bright colors and good lighting, shiny surfaces, and lofty towers that gleam in the sun. The bad guys usually have dark colors, thick, ugly walls, and surfaces that are pitted and scarred.

In both circumstances, a focus on simple building materials takes precedence, with walls of stone or wood, and simple forms that have few or no curves except in places that imply a high level of magic. For example, the architecture in high-magic areas may float in the air or have Escher-like geometry that allows players to walk on walls above the heads of their friends. Dungeons also get a lot of mileage in fantasy environments, with walls of rock or earth. Support beams are good to add, but they shouldn't get in the way of the player's progress through the level. For some reason, lava is also prevalent in both dungeons and evil lairs in the fantasy genre.

Finally, if you need to use technology, the fantasy cliché is to use an abundance of gears, pulleys, and levers to show how primitive the society is. This is true even if the machine in question performs some sort of miracle, like turning humble haberdashers into demonic Labrador retrievers.

Science Fiction

There are many different sci-fi architectural types. There are gritty, ultra-urban settings, exceedingly clean high-tech settings, spaceship interiors, small colonies on faraway planets, post-apocalyptic cities, and highly surrealistic alien vistas. Sci-fi environments are the most flexible of all the genres in terms of style, and you can do pretty much whatever you want. You just need to make sure there's evidence of "high tech" strewn about, whether it's the highly destructive equipment found in *Halo* or the storm troopers in the imperial garrisons of *Star Wars: Galaxies*. As long as the player is constantly reminded that he's in a sci-fi setting, he'll feel confident that he has a handle on your environment.

As in fantasy, there can be areas where the laws of physics are suspended or changed. However, in science fiction, it's important to show the player how this effect is being executed. Something as simple as a glow effect on the bottom of a floating platform is enough to satisfy most players.

Although good and evil exist in science fiction, the most extreme differences in environment tend to be divided along technological levels or socio-economic classes. Cleaner architecture and living spaces belong to the rich, while dirtier, rustier, more rundown areas belong to the poor. Simpler materials are used in rural settings, and higher tech materials are used in urban settings. A good example of this division is the *Star Wars* universe. The rich Empire surrounds itself with glossy surfaces and shining equipment, while the ragtag rebellion makes do with greasy, battered equipment in low-tech bases found in forest and arctic settings.

Period and Modern Settings

Games that take place in modern-day or historical settings share a basic rule: They're as true to their settings as the designers can make them. A game set in 18th Century France, for example, should use the architecture (or at least the architectural style) that existed at the time. Wild West settings, World War II settings, 1960s spy games, and action games set in the 1980s all need to be as faithful to those eras as possible, in order to provide maximum levels of immersion.

Furthermore, there will be a very vocal segment of your audience that will know (or *think* they know) more about the era of your game than you do. They'll be more than glad to point out any detail that deviates from the "true" flavor of the period, especially in historical games. This means that your research should be as complete as possible, even if you're just copying an architectural style rather than an environment that actually existed.

Modern-day settings are a little more lax than period settings. Since by definition you're already living in a modern-day setting, you'll unconsciously create architecture that's realistic for the current time period. You'll make slums appropriately rundown, and your business buildings will look appropriately corporate.

There's one danger that you'll face, however. If you're using modern-day architecture in something other than a mod, you might run into trademark infringement issues that can get you in trouble. If you use San Francisco's Transamerica Pyramid in your game, the people who own the building might want a part of your profits. And they might sue you over it if you don't get their permission in advance, whether they have the right to do that or not. Always keep in mind that people are sensitive, and businesses are always looking to protect (i.e. profit from) their properties, intellectual and otherwise. If you're not sure whether you're treading on anyone's property, either get legal advice from a professional or just don't do it in the first place.

Architecture and Fun

As with terrain, you should always build your environments with the enjoyment of the player in mind. The areas must be fun to move around in and help the gameplay.

Architecture has a benefit over open terrain because you can direct the player's movements much more easily. Buildings are also easy for players to identify as places for encountering conflict or finding information.

As stated earlier, the player's ability to move within the environment greatly influences how much fun he has. Blowing things up can be pretty fun, but if the player feels slow or weak in the way he moves, he'll put down the game in frustration.

Although the game engine largely determines the player's movement abilities, you want to avoid creating environments that frustrate the player, causing him to get stuck as he tries to navigate around your level. The player should be able to get around your halls and rooms easily. He should be able to move around your furniture and get through doorways without getting hooked on the doorjamb every time he tries to enter a new area.

Another way to frustrate a player is to make it hard for him to figure out where he is. Getting lost in a game is horribly unappealing, and you should try very hard to make your environments unique enough to give the player a sense of where he is at all times. Mazes are the exception to this rule, but unless it's a maze game, you can easily lose players by including them.

One of the easiest ways to generate geometry for architecture is to copy existing architecture again and again. Once you build one room or hallway section, if it's modular enough, it's pretty simple in most toolsets to clone it and move it down the hall. This is perfectly acceptable, as long as there's some sort of sign within each room to identify it as unique. It could be the color, a piece of furniture, or just a number on the door. As long as the player has at least a vague idea where he is and can get back to where he was, he won't get frustrated.

The next thing to consider is the gameplay of the engine you're using. Your architecture should facilitate this gameplay, whether it's a squad-based shooter like Red Storm's *Rainbow Six* games, a third-person fantasy hack-and-slasher like Blizzard's *World of Warcraft*, or a first-person shooter like Valve's *Half-Life*. The rooms should be big enough to circle-strafe, if that's appropriate, or should have enough room to fire a rocket launcher without blowing up the player as well. Ninety-degree corners are good for stealth games, where there's a way for players to peek around them, but they're easy to camp in on deathmatch maps.

Although real-time strategy games hardly ever take place inside buildings, consider the size of the force the player will want to bring into the space. Make sure you have enough room for the player to order his forces into some sort of formation, and that the biggest unit in the game can get through the door.

Linear Gameplay

When you're designing structures, it's easy to create *linear gameplay*. This just means that your level must be played in a certain order. The player goes from one room to the next, conquering each obstacle in the same order as every other player (see Figure 4.4).

In some cases, this type of gameplay makes sense. If you expect the player to go through the level only once and follow a certain storyline, linear gameplay will help you tell that story the way you want it to be told. However, linear gameplay means less choice and less freedom for the player, which can mean more frustration as the player must adjust to what **you** think is the best path for him to take to get through your game.

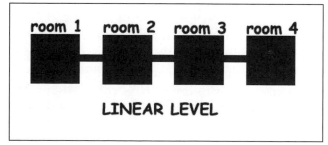

Figure 4.4 Simple linear level, where the player is shuffled from one encounter to the next.

Non-Linear Gameplay

In games that are meant for constant replay, like online first-person shooter maps, linear levels don't make much sense. For these types of games, having levels that allow for circular movement, with little or no interruption in the form of doors or locks, makes for much better gameplay (see Figure 4.5). The problem with non-linear levels is that every possible choice and action that the player might want to make has to be planned for, creating more and more work as you build in reactions for every possible action. Because of this, most non-linear games are actually partially linear.

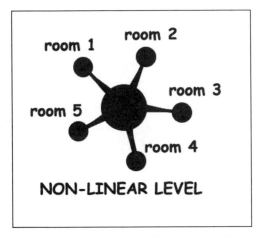

Figure 4.5 A simple non-linear level, where the player has an equal chance of going to any of the five rooms.

Tactics and Architecture

Just as it's important to consider the tactical ramifications of your terrain, the same is true of your architecture. How will the player use your structure to his benefit? How can you create interesting tactical puzzles for your audience?

Within a closed environment, a sniper can find a perch with a commanding view of the rest of the building, giving him a powerful advantage. In a hand-to-hand fight, a stairway can make all the difference in the outcome of a battle. A blind corner along a central pathway is an attractive place to set an ambush. A narrow hallway means a group uses a different formation than a wide hallway or even a large room. Always try to conceive of all the benefits and pitfalls that your structures present to the tactically minded player.

Another thing to think about is including additions to your architecture that appeal to several types of tactics. In Ion Storm's *Deus Ex*, the designers usually included at least two different paths to the player's goals, one path that appealed to the stealthy player and one to the aggressive, up-front player. This flexibility, as well as the other great design ideas, gave *Deus Ex* the stellar reputation it has now.

Texturing Architecture

Texturing architecture is a little more difficult than texturing terrain. With terrain, you tend to use textures in big sweeps, creating vast fields, craggy mountains, and everything in-between. You use as few textures as you can get away with, while still making the environment look good. With architecture, you'll want to have wall, floor, and ceiling textures, as well as textures for stairs, walkways, and any other conceivable surface you create. Unlike terrain, texturing room after room exactly the same will make your level look bland and uncreative. Although lighting can help individualize spaces, the textures you use will really bring your concepts into focus.

With architecture, you'll usually apply textures in much the same way you did with terrain. However, you'll want to apply them to individual surfaces, rather than to the whole object. First you choose the surface you want, and then you choose the texture you want to apply to it.

Sometimes, level editors will allow you to have layers of textures. This means you can lay one texture over another in order to blend the two. This is especially handy when you want to put a decal or sign on a wall without having to create your own texture. Just lay a brick texture on a surface, put a texture of graffiti on top of that, and you have a graffiti-covered brick wall.

Some engines allow you to create a transparent texture, so the player can see through the surface to the other side. This is very handy for objects like dirty windows or chain-link fences. If you tried to model every wire in a fence, it would be very expensive in terms of triangles. A flat surface with a transparent chain-link texture on it is vastly cheaper.

Tip

Always use textures that are appropriate for your level's theme. Don't use cinderblock or chrome textures in a fantasy environment, for instance. Also, some textures are more costly in terms of processor use than others. Reflective surfaces are very expensive, for example. A reflective surface has to monitor all the things it should be reflecting and replay them on its surface like a funhouse mirror. As you can imagine, a surface like this can drop your framerate quite a bit if it's overused.

Use textures instead of objects, when appropriate. If you have a number on a motel door, use a flat texture instead of creating a number object to stick to the door. Or, even worse, several unique doors, all with different numbers modeled into them.

Seams

Seams in your architecture occur when two objects don't fit really well together. As you run through your level, you'll see thin lines that let you look between objects and into the sky above or below, or into the room beyond. Remember, when you're placing things like walls and floors, it's perfectly acceptable to sink one into another to hide the seams.

However, try not to overlap objects. You might create a bug called *sorting*, which occurs when two objects are fighting to be seen by the player. If you place two walls in the exact same space, the player will see each wall's texture flash in and out as the game engine tries to figure out which texture is in front of which.

Collision

Collision is the force that keeps a player from passing through an object, or an object from passing through another object. Normally, the level editors that come with games create collision with the game's geometry. Sometimes, however, you might have to jump through hoops to get imported objects to have collision.

In structures, having bad collision is yet another way to lose points with reviewers. If the player's character runs next to a wall and his shoulder sinks into it as if it were made of air, you have a problem with your collision.

Fixing collision problems is probably a subject best left to an advanced level design book, since each game's toolset has different methods for rectifying them. If you find collision problems in your level, read any information you can find on your toolset, and see if others have overcome the same problem. Sometimes, it might be as simple as deleting the offending object and re-creating it, or it may involve building invisible collision walls to reinforce the walls you can see.

Putting It All Together

Creating architecture in games is much like carpentry. You have to figure out ahead of time how big you want everything, and you have to stick with those measurements. If you've ever tried to build anything from wood, you'll know what I mean. It's very easy to make lopsided rooms in games with tilted floors and ceilings that are too low. You'll find yourself making doors that go into nowhere, or are a few feet too high over the floor. It takes a careful eye and a lot of work to model a structure that doesn't look like a Salvador Dali painting. More than anything else you build, you need to have a map of the structure with fairly accurate measurements, in meters, noted for each room or hallway. "Measure twice, cut once" is a cliché that you should live by when making architecture.

It's also a good idea to make a few test levels before you try making the real thing. Run around inside them to find which rooms feel good, which feel too tight and which feel too big. Just plopping down a square 10' x 10' room and running around in it will give you a ton of information about how big you want to make your structure.

As always, remember that you're making your levels for others to enjoy, not for just yourself. Try to put function and gameplay before form and beauty. If the player is having enough fun, he won't notice that your architecture is a little bland or doesn't obey physical laws that much.

The Building of Prospero's Castle

The *Far Cry* Sandbox editor uses modular pieces to create architecture. Wall plates, floor plates, statues, and doors all can be put together, Lego-style, to create buildings. This makes creating architecture pretty easy, but it limits the level designer to using the existing pieces CryTek gives out. Either that, or you have to create the pieces in an external 3D modeling program, like Maya, and then import them into the game. For this example, I chose to use the available pieces.

Because *Far Cry* is a game about modern combat, the available pieces don't quite have the medieval feel I want, but I decide to make do and bring Prospero's Castle into the 21st century. This decision will help me later on, as well, since we'll be using mutants instead of zombies as the major enemy model.

Initially, I decide that I want to have a big building nestled inside an open volcano. Now, having to choose from either WWII bunker parts, modern-day super-lab parts, or ancient brick that looks like the set of an Indiana Jones film, I decide to make the castle a simple indoor structure placed inside the volcano. Therefore, I need to change the volcano a little to encompass the architecture I'm about to build. By raising the center a bit, I create a low volcano. The player can enter through a cave entrance, proceed through some interior areas, and then take an elevator to the top of the volcano, where Prospero awaits (see Figure 4.6).

Next, I start building the interior pieces. To start, I create a floor and walls (see Figure 4.7). In the *Far Cry* editor, it's kind of difficult to build things inside the terrain. I decide to build everything off to one side, and then I grab the whole thing and drag it into the volcano.

Before I go any further, I drag my interior into the volcano to make sure it fits. Luckily, it does. However, once I start building sections within this box, it's much too big to have fun in. It takes quite a while to run from one side to the other, and I realize that it will take a lot of zombies to fill the place up. I decide to make this interior a small

Figure 4.6 Volcano where Prospero's Castle is placed.

Figure 4.7 Floor and walls of Prospero's Castle.

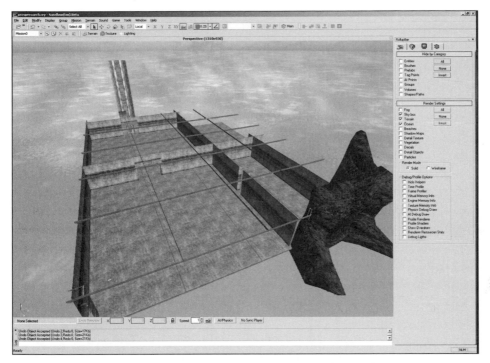

Figure 4.8 Looking through the back of the ceiling and the front wall.

three-room affair, with an entrance hall, a middle room, and a third room with an elevator shaft going up to the top of the volcano. I stick on a prebuilt cavern entrance that looks pretty cool, and now I'm ready to go to the next stage.

Most of the pieces I've used to build this are one-sided. In Figure 4.8, you're actually looking through backs of the ceiling and the front wall.

Next, I place a VisArea. Basically, this is an occluder that makes everything inside of it invisible to a player outside of it, and makes everything outside of it invisible to a player inside of it (see Figure 4.9). If the rooms were bigger, I would use one VisArea per room. The interior is pretty small, though, so I decide to use only one. Later, I might add more if there's a need. I then place a portal at the front entrance so a player can look inside the front entrance (and back out).

Now I select the entire interior and put them into one group. (When you group something, it glues all the pieces together so they act like one object.) I then move it all into the volcano. Using the Make Hole tool, I make some holes in the terrain to allow the player to move in and out of the interior (see Figure 4.10).

Figure 4.9 Volcano interior hidden by a VisArea. The area behind the cave entrance is shown slightly, as the portal does its job.

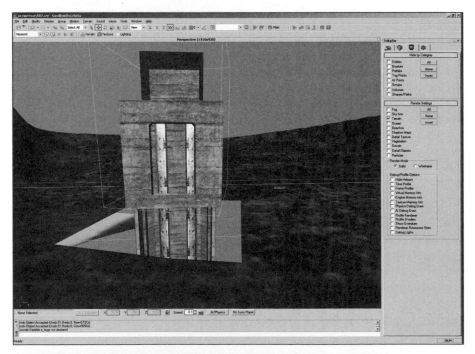

Figure 4.10 The elevator popping up through the hole in the volcano.

Then I realized that the cavern entrance has a brownish texture to it, while my volcano is more of a dark gray. Searching through the available textures, I can't find a good match to that texture. I decide to hide the cavern entrance with hanging vines, which actually ends up looking pretty nice (see Figure 4.11).

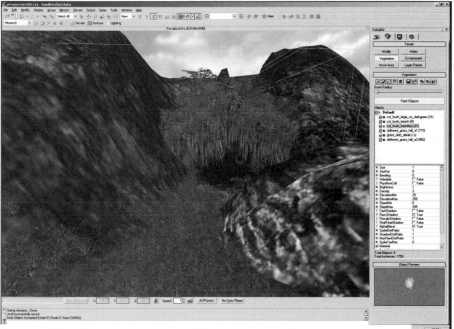

Figure 4.11 The cavern entrance hidden by hanging vines.

Once everything is placed, I put some architecture around the elevator shaft to hide all the one-sided pieces and the hole in the ground. I put an Easter Island-style head on top just for fun (see Figure 4.12).

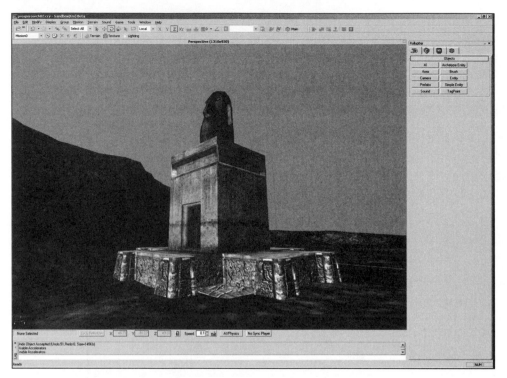

Figure 4.12 The finished elevator shaft.

What You Have Learned

In this chapter, you've learned about the following:

- The different tools you can use to make architecture, including brushes and tilesets.
- How game levels aren't sized exactly as the real world is, and you must scale them to create fun spaces.
- How real-world architectural design can teach you some lessons as a level designer.
- How to make your architecture more immersive.
- Some tips on how to create architecture for different genres.
- Texturing your architecture.

In the next chapter, we'll cover lighting and atmospheric effects, where we start to really make our architecture shine!

Review Questions

1. Why wouldn't a level that perfectly duplicates an average living room be fun for players?

2. How do architects encourage movement of people from one space to another within a building?

3. Why is texturing architecture more difficult than texturing terrain?

4. Name some standard features of a building in a fantasy genre game.

5. In what type of game would it be fun to have a building based on a painting by M.C. Escher?

On Your Own

1. Fire up the level editor of your choice and start fooling around with making and texturing buildings. Experiment with the different ways you can create simple and complex structures.

2. When you feel ready to build something, create a building that looks like a cute bunny. We'll call it the Trojan Bunny, after the one in the movie *Monty Python and the Holy Grail*. Make sure it's hollow and a game character can get in and out, and make sure there's a place where they can see through the bunny's eyes. Use portals or occluders.

3. Begin working on the architecture for your overall level. Remember to save the file continually. (Some level editors like to crash a lot when you're doing intensive work like this.) Remember to export frequently, and run around within the level to gauge how comfortable it feels to run from one place to another. Texture the architecture, and use portals and/or occluders to make sure your game isn't drawing anything the player wouldn't see, such as the terrain outside of the building the player is in that he wouldn't be able to see outside a window or doorway.

CHAPTER 5

LIGHTING AND ATMOSPHERIC EFFECTS

Establishing mood is an important part of immersing the player into your game. While architecture and terrain firmly establish in the player's mind where he is, you can help the player better understand the emotional impact of a place by enhancing its ambiance.

Definition

Ambiance: The special atmosphere or mood created by a particular environment. "The noir ambience is dominated by low-key lighting... and deep shadows, creating feelings of disorientation, loneliness and entrapment." (UCLA Film/TV Archive).

In this chapter, you'll learn about the following:

- Using lighting to add drama to your level
- Fog and haze
- Particle effects
- Using audio to add ambiance to your level

Lighting

Lighting is one of the designer's greatest tools to establish mood. With placement, intensity, color, and movement of light and shadows, you can really bring your level to life. The correct lighting can make an ordinary warehouse seem like a den of evil, make a tree seem like the personification of a benevolent god, or give a wintry chill to the most tropic of environments.

However, lighting is also an easy tool to misuse or abuse. It takes a subtle touch and a lot of knowledge to be able to use lighting to its fullest ability. In the movie industry, lighting a set is considered both an art and a science, and the people responsible for lighting train for many years to become good enough to work professionally.

Types of Lights

Three-dimensional modeling packages and level design tools usually have several different types of light sources you can use in your games. These lights can fall into two groups: static and dynamic lights.

- **Static lights** are rendered before the game begins. These lights often are termed by artists as *burnt in*, referring to the fact that they are actually part of the environment. Because they are rendered in advance, static lights are very cheap to use in games and are the best way to light most of the objects in your game.

- **Dynamic lights** exist within the game, generating light and shadows on the fly. Dynamic lights are much more natural looking than static lights because shadows and lighting effects are formed and evolve as movement happens within a scene. However, because the game engine is constantly calculating dynamic lighting, it is pretty expensive to use. When using dynamic lights, try to be as sparing with them as possible to save the hit on performance in your game.

Point Lights, Spotlights, and Directed Lights

Game engines and 3D modeling packages usually allow light to come from three different sources: point lights, spotlights, and directional lights.

- **Point**, or **ambient**, lights emit light in a 360-degree field. Sometimes called *fill lights*, they are used to light a scene generally. Dynamic point lights are the most expensive form of light.

- **Spotlights** are directed lights that usually show a discernable edge to where the light starts and stops. Spotlights are used mostly to highlight specific areas and objects that the designer or artist wants the player to notice. They can also be used to provide a source of light that does not really illuminate an area but provides a glowing landmark that can be seen easily in dark areas.

- **Directed lights** are basically soft spotlights. They don't have the harsh falloff of a spotlight, but they are still directed enough that they illuminate only small, specific areas. Directed lights are usually used to softly highlight areas or objects and accent already existing lighting.

Using Lights

As mentioned earlier, using lights to provide ambiance is an art and a science that can take many years to master completely. However, even an inexperienced designer can do a decent job at using lights to bring out the mood of a place.

The first thing to think about when placing lights, as always, is how they will affect the player's ability to work within your game environment. A completely dark game in which the player can't see his gun in front of his face can be very frustrating. Players don't particularly like feeling blind and become irritated at enemies that seemingly can see much better in the dark than they can.

This isn't to say that there isn't a place for games that have little to no light. The game *DOOM 3* by id Software uses a lack of light to intensify the player's feelings of vulnerability and horror. The *Thief* games by Looking Glass software and Ion Storm Games also use darkness to good effect to allow players to hide themselves in deep shadows.

However, horror and stealth games aside, it is usually very easy to underlight a game to make it more creepy or dramatic and then find that players can't see their enemies or even the door out of the place. Always try to err on the side of having too much light rather than having too little if you are having a hard time deciding how much to use.

The second thing to think about with lighting is how it makes a space feel. Lighting is a great way to set the mood of a space, and you'll want the correct mood to reinforce the other messages you are sending with your architecture and terrain. Three things to think about in terms of lighting and mood are color, position, and intensity.

- **Color theory** is one of the first classes you take when you try to get an art degree in college. It covers not only what colors go well together but also the psychological effect of different colors on people. Though a detailed discussion on color theory would be too long to fit in this book, the main thing you need to know about color is that blues make an environment feel cold, and red and orange make an environment feel warm. Using a blue-colored light can really enhance the feeling that your secret lair level is really in the arctic, while a red, orange, or sometimes purplish light can turn an otherwise bland cabin into a warm sanctuary against the cold.

- **Positioning** of your light can enhance the drama of an environment. Actually, the light isn't what causes an area to become more dramatic; it's the shadows the light casts. Shadows give the viewer a lot of information: whether the object being seen is flat or three-dimensional, where light is coming from, and how strong that light source is. A shadow can also outline whatever's casting it, allowing an object to stand out in relief from its background. All of this information is controlled by the position of a light source.

A high position from the front of an object can erase details and flatten an object, making it seem more mundane or ordinary. Position the light to the side, and details leap into stark relief. A light from behind means you are now looking at a shadowy silhouette, steeped in mystery. Lights from below or right above cause strange shadows and highlights to appear, making objects and people seem alien or scary or, if done right, filled with divine power. When lighting your areas, experiment a lot with light positions to see how it can really change the mood of your game.

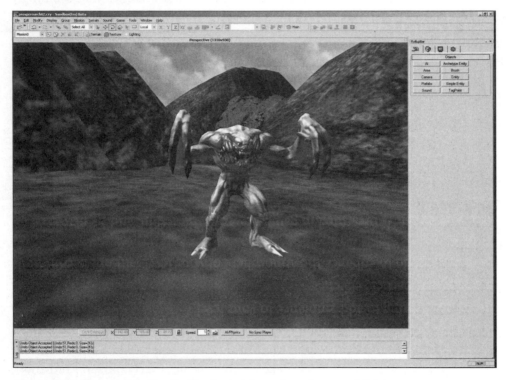

Figure 5.1 A mutant in *Far Cry* illuminated from above in normal light.

- **Intensity** of the light can determine the impact a light source has on an object. High intensity can wash out the colors, while low intensity can shroud an area in gloom. Usually, the more focused a light is, such as a spotlight, the higher its intensity. In games, you'll usually use lights of medium intensity, with spots and directed lights to increase intensity on specific items to help them stand out.

Figure 5.2 The same mutant, now lit from beneath with a dynamic light. Spoooooky.

Fog and Haze

Atmospheric effects such as fog and haze can really add ambiance to a level. However, more importantly, they help the game engine become more efficient.

Fog and other atmospheric effects blur out or obscure objects that are some distance away. This effect can make an area seem mysterious or creepy. Players become nervous when they can't see as far as they're used to, and depending on the thickness of the haze, this can slow them down as they try to make sure that their next step isn't a fatal one.

Fog is also helpful in game engines because the engine doesn't have to draw what the player can't see. With a thick fog that allows the player to see only 50 feet ahead, everything beyond that distance doesn't have to be drawn.

Other atmospheric effects such as ground fog or clouds (in flying games) are also good for promoting certain types of ambiance, but they usually don't have the same benefits as an all-encompassing fog. Because of this, effects like these are pretty expensive in terms of processor use, especially if they are moving.

Particle Effects

By far the glitziest way to create ambiance in a game is through the use of particle effects. Particle effects can range from a smoking fire to a swarm of bees to a waterfall to a roving gang of post-apocalyptic thugs. Anything that involves the coordinated movement of many identical objects can be created using a particle system within a game.

Particle effects, like dynamic lights, are extremely expensive on the processor. In fact, anything that moves is expensive on processors. With particles, the engine is continually generating particle after particle, subjecting each particle individually to whatever forces it's programmed to apply to them (such as gravity or wind) and then taking away the particle and starting fresh with a new one. Because of this, it's best to use particle effects sparingly and to not clump them into one place.

However, particle effects can really cap off an area in terms of ambiance. A few well-placed torches in a medieval castle, a bubbling fountain in the center of a corporate reception area, or flies hovering around a corpse can do a great job of immersing a player in your world.

Using particle effects in retail game-editing tools is usually pretty easy. The toolset will usually have a few of them that you can plop down and fool around with. Usually, these are the standards, such as fires of different sizes and maybe swarms of some kind of unidentifiable bug. There may be some water effects, too, such as a waterfall or a stream. There might even be some special objects with particle effects attached, such as a torch or a fountain.

However, importing your own particle effects is usually a fairly difficult, if not impossible, task so you might not have a lot of effects to choose from beyond those used in the original game.

Audio

Three senses are used when playing video games. The primary sense used is sight: Video games are by far a visual medium. Another sense used is touch, or the tactile sense, which currently is limited to primitive force feedback techniques that rarely bring a true sense of immersion into a game. Finally, there is sound.

Using correct sounds for environments tremendously increases the amount of immersion a player feels. Nothing makes the sea more real than the sound of rushing waves, makes a jungle come alive more than the sounds of rustling trees and the call of the native animals, or makes a spooky old house more creepy than the creaking of its old floorboards and the slamming of its shutters in the wind.

As a level designer, you may or may not have a lot of control over what sounds go where. Usually, sounds are attached to different objects in the game, such as a generator giving off engine noises or a fountain making water sounds. Sounds such as night noises, rushing water, and the like can be dropped into a level just like an object. The invisible object will transmit whatever sound it's linked to in an unending loop that starts whenever the player gets within a certain radius of the sound object.

Using Audio

Ambient audio is an easy thing to overuse. Have you ever played a game where you had to turn down the sound effects or music because you couldn't hear the voice lines? Or because the sound effects became repetitive and annoying? The designers of those games thought they were putting in something that would immerse the player, and for a couple minutes, it probably did. Then, it all went wrong.

In the real world, ambient sound is always present. Right now, I hear the fans in my computer and my especially clicky keyboard. (I like clicky keyboards.) When I go outside, I hear wind and car sounds and my footsteps. How much of this do I pay attention to? Hardly any of it. We unconsciously prioritize and filter out all the noise we don't want to listen to and pay attention only to noises that are unexpected or that call out to us specifically, such as a car rushing in our direction or someone calling out our name.

In games, you have to take the fact that ambient audio is expected but isn't necessarily wanted. It has to be subtle and quiet. It also has to fit the environment perfectly, or players will notice it and hate it almost immediately. For example, the player enters a dark forest at night. In the background, a songbird (a notoriously diurnal type of critter) is twittering happily. Players will notice immediately that it doesn't belong (part of that subconscious prioritization thing) and, after figuring out that it's harmless, will shove it into the "things I hate about this game" bin.

Another important thing to consider about ambient audio is that it needs to be consistent without becoming repetitive. If you have ambient audio for one thing the player expects to hear (such as a fountain giving off water noises), then all fountains should have noise. However, different fountains should produce different sounds, just as they do in real life. Further, if all fountains have noise, then other things that make noise, such as trees rustling in the wind and swarms of insects, should also make noise. You need a noise for practically everything! With all the sounds you need, it's no wonder that in many games audio takes up as much of the storage space as the art, or more.

Music in games is also a touchy issue with players. Usually, players would rather supply their own music over having to listen to your choices. However, the presence of music can add a cinematic feel to your game that can increase immersion as well as cover up a lack of quality sound effects.

Music is usually presented in a couple of different ways:

- **Music by zone.** Some games require the level designer to link music files with specific areas of the game. This could be one set of music for an entire level, or several areas within the level that are triggered when the player enters them. Placing music like this can give the players forewarning of impending combat, or link a certain type of function to a place. For example, if you have the same melody play whenever there is a healing spring nearby, the player will very quickly link that music to the healing function. In this way, you don't even have to make every healing spring look the same: Just play the song and, like Pavlov's dogs, the player will come running for some hit point regeneration.

- **Music by action.** Many games link music to certain types of action. This allows for a more appropriate song to be played as the level of action increases and decreases during the course of the game. This requires a great level of skill to pull off well, as each song needs to blend into one another perfectly and seamlessly as they gain or lose tempo or change to a different theme. The beauty of this type of music is that the level designer doesn't have anything to do with it: just sit back and let the music play.

- **Music by choice.** Many console games now come with "Radio Stations" that the player has control over. The XBox, in fact, has a built-in MP3 player that allows the player to build soundtracks from his own collection of music. This allows players the ultimate freedom in determining the amount of music they want with their game. The upside is, once again, you don't really have to worry about it. The downside is that the game might lose some cinematic power when the player racks up the greatest hits of "Air Supply."

Example: Lighting the Subterranean Rooms Under the Volcano

This is a really short example. If you have *Far Cry* and are opening up the example levels, this will be a bit more useful for you if you go on in and look at the lights we're placing.

Because *Far Cry* uses dynamic lights only for interior spaces, we'll need to be frugal with placing them. Placing lights in *Far Cry* is as easy as placing everything else—just drag and plop. We'll put one dynamic light in each of the big rooms.

For those of you who can open up the example, we'll make one light red and one light blue. Notice how different each of the rooms feels. Color theory at work!

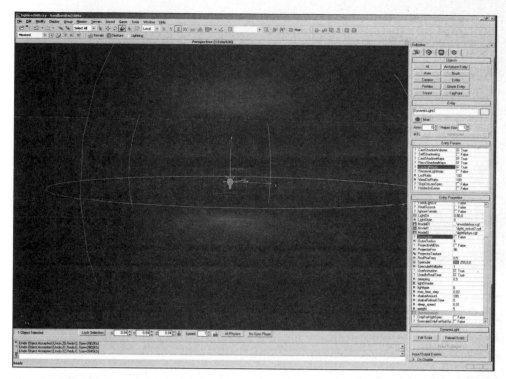

Figure 5.3 Placing a dynamic light in one of the rooms in our level. Notice the circle around the light. It shows how far the main strength of the light goes.

What You Have Learned

In this chapter, you learned:

- The difference between static and dynamic lights
- About spot, point, and directed lights
- How to use lighting to add ambiance to your level
- About fog and particle effects
- How to use audio to enhance the atmosphere of your level without becoming annoying
- Three ways music is presented in games: by zone, by action, and by player choice

Review Questions

(answers in Appendix C)

1. What two types of lights are available to use in games?

2. What are the three forms each light may take?

3. Name three types of particle effects.

4. Name the three senses that games provide stimulus for.

5. Why is fog good for your game?

On Your Own

1. Using your toolset, begin playing with lights. This usually is more fun in FPS games, but it can still be good with top-down games such as RTSs. Experiment with changing the color of the lights, the placement, and any other controls that your toolset gives you.

2. While you're at it, see if you can drop in some ambient sounds. This might take a while to figure out, since placing sounds is usually not the most important thing people want to do with editors.

3. Try playing with the fog plane, if there is one. Many toolsets, especially RTSs, don't use them.

4. Finally, place some particle effects. Try some flames or smoke emitters to see what they look like. Put a bunch of them in one place and see how much that affects performance.

CHAPTER 6

PLACING ENCOUNTERS

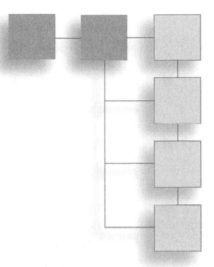

Terrain is beautiful, and architecture is nice, but if there is nothing to interact with, your players will soon grow bored. The biggest attraction of video games is that the player is not just a displaced and placid viewer. If he wanted to play a game where he just sat back and let you entertain him, he would have rented a movie instead.

Encounters take many forms. There are passive encounters that sit and wait for the player to come to them, and there are active encounters that search out the player wherever he may be hiding. Passive encounters can take the form of a lock on a door or a peasant standing in a field waiting for the player to walk by and ask him the time of day. Active encounters can be armed enemies doing a room-by-room search of a base or one player meeting another in a massively multiplayer game. Whatever the encounter may be, these will determine the flavor and potency of your gameplay more than any other facet of your level.

Placing encounters is usually pretty easy compared to making terrain and architecture but can take a lot more time to get just right before your level is ready to be played. In most toolsets, placing an encounter is as simple as that: dragging them from a list and placing them on your map to await the player's arrival.

However, just placing encounters doesn't mean that you have created fun. Placing encounters takes a lot of thought to make them appropriate for the situation the player is in.

In this chapter, you'll learn the following:

- How to place encounters
- Different types of encounters, such as informational, puzzle, and combat

- How to place the player and encounters within your level for maximum impact
- Formational tactics and how to place enemies so they look like they know what they're doing
- How to place items so that your player always feels like he's on a treasure hunt while still having all the equipment he needs to survive

Informational Encounters

An informational encounter is one where you use an interactive object such as an NPC peasant or anything that can communicate to impart information to the player in a computer game. This information could include knowledge of your game world, answers to riddles, or lessons on how to play the game better. Most games with no story element involved, such as a lot of puzzle or racing games, just pop up a text panel to tell the player what the game developer wants him to know. In games that are more story based, imparting information is generally given to the player both in a pop-up text panel and in game encounters.

If you're placing encounters that give out information, remember that players need time to understand the information. This means that the knowledge you are giving must be presented in a way in which the player can take whatever time he needs to absorb it. If the player is being harried by an endless stream of abominable snowmen, he really doesn't have the time to learn how the Tibetan monks believe that the holy scriptures inside the Sacred Cave of the Platinum Yak hold the answer to the Meaning of Life. Try to keep informational encounters away from action encounters. Also, you'll want to set up the knowledge so that the player can repeat it at any time in case he forgets it or feels he needs to clarify something.

If the information you want the player to know is vital to his success in the game, it is better to place this information where the player can't avoid it. Put the information in a text box during level load or in a cutscene of some sort. Don't leave it up to the player to find this type of information by himself or he'll miss it every time.

If some information is important but not vital for the player to know, try to put that information in bottlenecks, where it will be hard for the player to miss. Put the old miner who knows a clue to why the ghost is spooking the settlers of Spartan 8 by the only opening to the next encounter. If you want to be really aggressive, script the miner so that he greets the player when the player comes near. A word of warning, however: The more aggressive you make this type of thing, the more the player will try to avoid it.

If the information is nice to know but not vital to the understanding or completion of the game, make a mini-game of slightly hiding the information. Put the information in a newspaper lying on the ground that the player can read when he picks it up and activates it. Or give the information to friendly NPCs wandering about the level in out-of-the-way places. With this type of information, it is best not to be heavy hand-ed in its delivery. No one likes being subjected to a three-minute cutscene that gives trivial and useless information. Keep it on a need-to-know basis, where the curious who need to know can get it and the players who couldn't care less can skip by it with-out becoming annoyed at a halt in their progress.

Puzzle Encounters

Puzzles in most story-based games are usually just a form of lock. The player generally can't move further into the game without first solving it or is prevented from accessing a reward of some type until the puzzle is solved.

Puzzles are usually placed at bottlenecks so that the player can't help but come across them. They also should be as obviously connected to their reward as a lock is obvi-ously attached to a door. Having a button with no apparent effect within the sight of the player makes it hard for the player to figure out what exactly it does. This can be pretty hard to do sometimes because you don't want to make things too easy, and you also have the problem of never knowing where the player is facing. Most games take control away from the player for a second and do a quick cutscene showing what the effect of the button is. The game *Prince of Persia: Sands of Time* does this to good effect. You could also show the effect on a mini-map or launch a voiceline telling the player what he has done, if these avenues are appropriate to your game.

Like informational encounters, puzzles that require concentration should be in areas that have little or no interruption. It might be a great image in your head, the player constantly fighting off foes while trying to figure out the mechanism keeping him from accessing the gold mine of ol' Joe the Pirate, but to a player, it will stop being fun very quickly. If you have to keep throwing enemies at the player, do it at a reduced rate so that he has a little more time to think between action encounters.

When making professional games, you are often required to have a variable degree of difficulty for each level. In cases where your game needs you to prepare easy, medium, and hard levels, a puzzle or a riddle is the hardest thing to scale appropriately. An easy enemy might be defeated in one hit, and a hard enemy might take five, but who can determine which of three riddles is the hardest, especially for a player who has no talent with them in the first place? Plus, programming each of those circumstances into your level can be a difficult task. In these circumstances, many designers would just forget about the puzzle and go for a bloodlock. This might be the easiest option, but it certainly will not get you points for creativity. Perhaps you could give a variable level of hints previous to a riddle so that the easy player has a lot of clues to help him, but the hard player has very few or none. A more physical puzzle might have a time limit, where the door it opens is open only for a certain time before it closes.

Lock Puzzles

Locks, obviously, are mechanisms that prevent things from easily accessing places. They can prevent people from going into rooms, bears from getting into the campsite cooler, or water from getting into the Panama Canal. Locks are a staple of modern games, being used frequently to keep players in one place until they find the key, whether it be a physical or mental one. Placing locks in the right places can help your game feel more consistent.

The first rule of lock placement is to try and not place locks on places that can be circumnavigated. This is pretty obvious: If you want a lock to work, don't leave a back door open into the same room. However, it is perfectly okay to have that open back door if you make getting to that door as difficult for the player as getting through that lock. Allowing the player to solve the riddle of Thoth to get into the vault of the pharaohs or letting him go into the dangerous tunnel filled with deadly, poisonous cranes will make the player feel as if he has a lot more freedom than he actually does. One tip, however: If the player successfully answers the riddle, don't make him go through the tunnel. Games that suggest you have a choice and then give you no choice at all can anger players. On the other hand, don't suddenly make that tunnel inaccessible or get rid of all the encounters in it. Some players will want to try their mettle on those cranes just for a sense of completion.

When using locks, remember that anything that halts a player's progress is pretty frustrating for the player. Unless your game is presented as having a lot of puzzle solving in it, players will get frustrated if they have to take time out of their frenzied action to sit around and figure out what combination of teal-, ochre-, and peach-colored buttons they are supposed to press to get to the next part of the game. The faster the gameplay of your level, the easier it should be to unlock doors, up to and including little cutscenes showing the door that needs to be unlocked and the key mechanism for it before sending the player into the big room filled with machine gun-toting cockroaches from the planet Kazoog.

Bloodlocking

Some locks are not encounters at all but conditions. Frequently, a designer will create a scenario where the player has to defeat x number of foes before he can progress to the next level. This is referred to lovingly in the industry as "bloodlocking." It is kind of a design cliché and frowned upon by designers in an intellectual sense, but it is such an easy condition to program into a level that it finds its way into most combat-oriented games. Other conditional locks could be to herd x number of platypi, collect x number of electrum coins, or create a city with x gpu.

When using conditions that bar progress, you have to make sure the player knows what is expected of him. In a lot of games, this is done as a "mission briefing" or "list of objectives" presented to the player at the beginning of a level. Usually, the player even has a HUD function that allows him to pop up a list of his pending and completed level objectives so that he knows what still needs to be done.

Often, conditions can seem like spoilers. As a designer, you'll want to surprise the player with an encounter, but putting a mission objective like "defeat Captain Gernerder" when the player thought he killed Gernerder in level 3 might be less fun than having him spring up and change the nature of the entire level. In cases like these, you'll want to update your conditions list mid-level. When doing this, make sure you update the player's condition list and then give him some visual sign that the terms of winning have changed. Most toolsets should give you this ability, but keep an eye out for it if the toolset you are using doesn't allow it.

Movement Puzzles

Designing movement puzzles usually takes place in the terrain and architectural steps of building a level, but we'll talk about it here for the sake of completeness.

Some genres of games focus entirely on having the player use his avatar's ability to move and jump to get through the game. Normally called platformers, games like Nintendo's *Mario* and Sega's *Sonic the Hedgehog* games have the player running and jumping over all sorts of obstacles in order to progress through the game.

Designing games like these is usually a vastly different process than normal level design. There usually is a lot more emphasis on paper design, where every aspect of the level is drawn out on graph paper. Artists take those designs and create them in a 3D environment.

Most 3D games, however, add some movement puzzles into their mix of combat just to keep things interesting. Games like *Tomb Raider* and *Indiana Jones* games have a good mix of combat, puzzle solving, and movement challenges.

When designing movement puzzles such as jumping puzzles, timing puzzles, and obstacle races, you should be very certain of the movement abilities of the player's avatar. You should know exactly how far it can jump, how fast it can move, how tightly it can corner, and how responsive the game is to the player's needs. This will require you to test the game over and over to determine whether your movement challenges are viable and fun.

Similarly to locks, movement puzzles are very disrupting to the flow of your game if you are mixing them in with combat or racing action. Nothing is more frustrating than a long, drawn-out jumping puzzle set right in the middle of a fast-paced action game. Your movement puzzles should be set at the same speed as the rest of the gameplay. Keep challenges short: A 30-minute jumping puzzle that can stretch out to an hour if the player is less than skillful is generally a fun killer. In fact, a jumping puzzle that lasts more than two minutes should be looked at carefully to make sure that it isn't killing the player's momentum.

Timing puzzles, where the player has to wait for the right moment to act to get past the puzzle, are also pace killers. A player will have to stop, pay attention, get ready, and act to defeat a timing puzzle such as the old swinging pendulum trap. Timing puzzles are definitely the kind of puzzle you should stay away from in fast-paced games unless they are crucial to a mission's success. Shooting a barrel on a conveyor belt just as it passes a group of guards to blow it up in their faces is a good example. The player doesn't need to do it, but it helps his progress, so it rewards him with a cool way to get past a few enemies.

In fact, having incidental puzzles, such as a row of rocks where the player can jump from one to another just to see if he can, will help to expand the playability of your levels. Remember, while you are trying to create a fun experience for players, there is no way you can successfully make the play experience as intense for one person as you can for another. By placing trivial challenges, interesting tactical puzzles, side quests, and mini-games, you can increase the chances that players will find something they really enjoy about your game. One note, however: When making trivial side puzzles, be absolutely sure to reward the player for completing it. Put a power-up or similar reward at the end so that players don't feel they've wasted their time.

Active Encounters and Combat

Combat is the primary game mechanic available to you in most of today's games. As a player, you are given the chance to defeat horrible monsters, the undead, space aliens, gang members, terrorists, and any other conceivable foe. While violence in video games is a common topic among political pundits and "parental" groups, a quick look at any mass media will find that it is a common theme. The trick is to make sure that any violence in the game serves a purpose. Are you just placing 400 gib-monsters for the sake of lots of gratuitous violence, or are they there for a reason—protecting something or trying to get to something? Even if you do want lots of gratuitous violence, having a reason for it always makes it more compelling. If it's just non-stop killing, it gets really tiresome.

One word of caution: If you are working on a massive "A" title that's hopefully going to sell millions, or even a little indie project that you're just doing for school, be prepared to take heat from numerous people if you go over the top with violence, and especially graphic depictions of the violence. Whether it's that delightfully idealistic group on campus, or Mothers Against Fictional Violence, it will likely happen.

Placing Enemies

Placing enemies will probably be one of the easiest things you do when making a level if a game's enemy AI is good. The following are some things to remember when placing enemies in your game.

Know your game's limitations. Moving characters is one of the most processor-intensive things you can do in a game. With artificial intelligence coupled with movement animations, plus having to check for collision so the unit won't walk through a wall to get at the player, a computer's processor gets severely taxed when these guys start running around. Always find out the limit of your game engine's abilities, and make sure to stay well under them. If a game's toolset manual says to keep under 15 enemies per level, use only 10 to 12. Although you can probably stuff 20 enemies in there, your frame rate will suffer enough to make it unplayable for a lot of players with older machines.

Know your game's strengths and weaknesses. Often, you can stick more enemies into a level as long as they are the same enemy. Having to draw 10 different models, all with different animations, AIs, and textures, is much more draining on a processor than 15 clones.

Far Cry, as an example, even on lower settings, can start to show some serious frame rate hits just with four or five enemies onscreen, especially when using "explosive" weapons. The combination of animations, high pixel particle effects, and special graphics techniques like shine and bumpiness can quickly add up to make a very taxing environment.

Neverwinter Nights on the other hand, because it relies as much on the environments and simpler models and textures, on a decent machine can allow for a dozen kobolds all chasing after the player with a minimal impact.

One other concept to understand is activation and deactivation of entities. Through this sort of behind-the-scenes AI manipulation, even if your game has a hard limit of no more than four enemies on the level, you can make the player believe he is traveling through a level with hundreds of crazed monks riding their saddled flamingos, even though they never actually see more than four on the screen at once. With limitations as strict as the ones mentioned here, extremely careful use of geometry, combined with activation and deactivation of entities, becomes critical to maintain the illusion of having far more enemies in a level than there are. Activation and deactivation are usually as simple as the game telling an actor to turn "on" or "off" after something happens, whether a trap is triggered, or the player comes within 100 feet of the actor that is about to become active.

Some games are made for large conflicts, with the player fighting many units, and some games are meant for the player to fight only one or two. You might be able to have 20 monsters fighting the player in a Croteam's *Serious Sam* level but only a couple in a Diversion Entertainment's *One Must Fall* battle.

Real Time Strategy (RTS) games, and any other game where the players rely on a set of resources to increase their forces, should take those resources into account when placing AI spawn points. The AI should be placed as close to a source of resources as the player is, or else you are giving him an unfair disadvantage (or advantage, if you are placing him closer). Players appreciate fairness and will be disappointed if they catch you making the game easier on them. Besides, that's what cheat codes are for, right?

A *spawn point* is a point where the level designer has told the game to create new objects, usually mobile ones such as enemies, friendly units, or wildlife. This creation process can usually be modified to spew out objects in a number of different patterns. You can have a set number of things pop out or an infinite supply, only one unit at a time or many, at any rate, from one per second to one per eon.

Also for RTS games, try to place enemies near enough that the player can find them pretty quickly. Having to search the map for 15 minutes is boring and frustrating and allows the AI's superior force-building ability to flourish, letting it grow to a maximum-sized force if it hasn't already spread across the map by that time.

For story-oriented RTS play, it often makes sense to have enemies strung along the path you want the player to follow. Little pockets of enemies can help to flesh out your world and make it seem more of a living, breathing world while the player travels to the "meat" of your design.

For first- and third-person action games, enemies are usually pretty expensive to have a lot of. In some games, an enemy will come into existence only when a certain condition has been met. This is called "spawning" an object. Using a script, you'll be able to pop enemies into existence when the player gets within a certain range (hopefully, a range near enough to be close, but far enough that the player can't see them popping into thin air). Coupling this with activating and deactivating enemies, as covered previously, will go far to stretch out how many mobile objects you can stuff into your level.

Placing enemies is a waste if the player doesn't get to encounter them. If you have Jed the Mad Slasher over in the corner of our level somewhere, only explorer types of players will ever see him. Most players will probably walk from encounter to encounter without ever deviating from the main path. Like puzzles, if you have a situation that you absolutely must have the player encounter, put it someplace on the main path where it can't possibly avoided, or inform the player directly where he needs to go to find what you need him to find. This can be as simple as having a glowing dot on a minimap or as complex as having someone on the main path specifically approach the player with a quest, such as an expedition to find a can of soda from a mystical vending machine or to hunt for a comrade who has strayed into some forgotten warehouse and needs rescuing (or a decent burial). Quests like this are handy when you want to encourage exploration, because the player can explore beyond the object of the quest, giving a less linear feel to the game world.

Of course, the length and complexity of a puzzle like this should make sense for the type of game you're making. Obviously, for a fast-paced, action-packed shoot-em-up, keep it short and sweet, probably involving a daring rescue with lots of flying bullets. For an RPG, a longer journey with some hints at further mysteries might be just the ticket.

Placing the Player

First impressions are very important. Where the player begins sets the mood for the level and will influence how the player will approach the challenges laid out for him. If you make the initial area generic, you risk losing the player's interest. If you make it interesting, the player feels more motivated to see what this fascinating new environment has in store.

Some levels suggest starting points more than others. If the player is entering a dungeon with a definite beginning and end, placing the spawn point is pretty easy. More open-ended levels, especially outdoor levels, require a bit more thought.

The first thing to consider when placing the player's spawn point is to put it in a place where the player has some time to acclimatize to his surroundings. The player should be able to get a good look at some major landmarks so that he can orient himself if he gets lost. Remember, the spawn point is the first point the player will think of when trying to triangulate his position if he gets turned around. While it doesn't have to be a big sign that says, "Hey! You spawned right here!" in big, bright neon lights, it should be a fairly unique place with a decent view of any large structures or hills. In levels that are all interior, make the spawning room exceptional in some way so that the player will recognize it if he ends up walking in circles.

Tip

When spawning the player, make sure he's facing the way you want him to face. This might seem obvious, but it's the kind of thing that is easy to forget. Players will generally walk straight forward from the position they spawn, without turning around. Give them a nudge in the right direction by facing them where you want them to go.

The surroundings of the spawn point should also indicate two things: the nature of the level's environment and what the player needs to do next. If you want the player to go to a radio tower before he goes to a bunker, put the spawn point where the player has a good view of the tower but can't see the bunker yet. Action also gives a good indication of what to do next. A fierce firefight a hundred yards ahead, with the occasional Tomahawk missile flying merrily overhead, usually tells the player where he should go first.

In RTS games, placing the spawn point of the player and his opponents should take even more thought. The spawn area should always be in a relatively easy place to defend so that he has a chance to fend off a rush while he builds up his forces.

Placing the AI

First and foremost when actually placing your AIs, remember that in the real world, there's usually a reason why everything is where it is. In making a game, you might not have to give each and every creature or enemy a reason to be there, but if you know in your own mind why they are there, it makes it easier to place them in a way that looks and feels more natural. If there's a heavily guarded base, chances are that troops will be stationed at guard towers, major entrances, and of course just lounging, either in offices or at the barracks. Unless an alarm has been triggered, it makes no sense for every single troop to be on high alert, waiting for the player to show up and kill them.

By imparting a sense of continuity and realism to your environment, you accomplish two major goals. First off, the player will feel a sense of recognition in the environment, and you won't have to work so hard at telling him where to go next. Secondly, the player will become even more immersed when he feels the atmosphere is "real," rather than just some stage setup to get him from point A to point B.

Formations

Formations are one of the most interesting placement tools you can use because even though they don't necessarily do much to make the AI any smarter, they do a lot for the player's feeling of immersion. When in a first-person shooter, the assumption is usually that you're going up against a lot of military-trained foes. They tend to use formations and tactics very heavily in how they perform their duties. Placing them in formation or, if the game allows for it, encouraging them to move in formation can do a lot to make the player feel like he really is infiltrating a heavily guarded compound that is protected by actual trained mercenaries instead of a bunch of dumb AIs.

Types of Formations—Some Fire Team Examples

First, a quick definition. A fire team usually consists of four members: the team leader, the automatic rifleman, and two additional riflemen.

- **Team Leader:** Provides direction and issues commands to his unit. Also usually positioned to make sure that the automatic gunner can support in the most efficient manner possible, depending on the scenario.
- **Automatic Rifleman:** The main firepower in any unit. Usually positioned so that he can provide for any flank, as well as receive assistance from the first rifleman.
- **First Rifleman:** Primarily there to make sure the automatic rifleman can keep going by providing new magazines and keeping the automatic rifle going.
- **Second Rifleman:** Most simply put, the point man. He is positioned in the area most likely to encounter action to provide the earliest possible warning to the rest of his team.

Wedge

The wedge (see Figure 6.1) provides some natural coverage for every member, as well as maintains visual contact with each member of the unit. No one member obstructs the view of another, so that the whole team can communicate clearly and quickly without breaking formation.

Column

This is very useful for standard patrol routes and narrower hallways. (Column formation is shown in Figure 6.2.) It allows each member to maintain visual contact while providing natural cover for all members from his quadrant. The automatic gunner also has a clear line of sight without endangering the second rifleman.

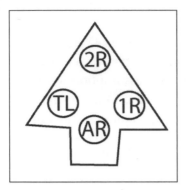

Figure 6.1 Wedge formation.

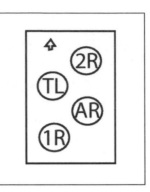

Figure 6.2 Column formation.

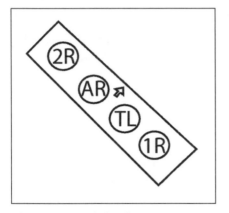

Figure 6.3 Echelon formation.

Echelon

The echelon (see Figure 6.3) is a lateral column specifically used for wide patrol routes and especially useful on high alert. It places the four members of the fire team nearly shoulder to shoulder, making it easy for one or more members in the center to pivot and watch behind while maintaining full visual contact to the front as well. The biggest advantage of this formation is that no one member gets in the line of fire of another, but each team member also provides no easy cover for other members of the team.

Spawning versus Static Placement

If you've played massively multiplayer games before, take a second to get the concept of spawning as you know it out of your head. That's not what we're talking about here. In this case, the concern is how many actors you have up at any given moment. If you statically place every single entity in your level, and the game can't intelligently shut them down if a player is out of range, you could possible make the level unplayable just because the CPU is spending all its time updating 400 different AI actors. Spawning actors as you need them can do a lot to help this kind of problem, but it can't be used in all scenarios. If you have a very non-linear level, you have no real way of knowing when the player will get to a specific location. One way to handle this is through the use of *trigger regions*. As soon as the player crosses the trigger, you can choose that time to spawn the enemies. If the player triggers spawns in every location of the map and then kills them, you could still run into the same problems, but at some point you have to hope the player actually plans on killing some of those actors. In addition, once the player crosses out of that trigger region again, you can always despawn any actors left if you're that concerned about performance problems.

Item Placement

You have your mix of static and spawned enemies placed throughout your level. It's 30 minutes of non-stop carnage and gunfights. Thank God for unlimited ammo! Oh, wait, there's no unlimited ammo? Well, that's why you want to make sure you have a good idea of what it takes to kill a platoon of insane wolverines and then polish off the head penguin berserker. Placement should make sense in the overall scheme of the game, such as health packs and a little armor in a barracks or a med center, a bunch of ammo and a new Nerf® gun in the armory. Be generous with health, armor, and ammo, but don't go overboard. You still want your level to be challenging, right?

Remember to think of every item type you might need to place. Armor, weapons, ammo, health and/or mana packs, keys, tools, special objects, treasure, vehicles (if appropriate), upgrades, power ups, and even the occasional nostril enhancer.

When placing items, make sure the important items, like health, ammunition, or items that the player will require to progress to the next level, are easily seen. Put them near the main path where the player is most likely to go. Anything extra can and should be put in out-of-the-way places to reward the player for the extra exploration it took to find them. A good ratio would be to put 75 percent of your health packs and ammo and 100 percent of the necessary, plot-hinging items in easy to find places and the rest in hidden caches.

Another type of item placement is resource placement in RTS games. You should always place a good amount of all types of resources near where the player's forces will spawn. Other resources should be carefully placed in areas in places about halfway between opponents in strategically weak areas. If you want a longer playing map, a good way to help the player get to higher levels of power more quickly is to place a secondary allotment of resources outside the player's immediate line of sight, but still close enough to expand to easily.

Growth/Challenge Curve

Growth and the challenge curve in a game are always the hardest things to balance. If you have a standard curve of difficulty and you've followed that curve faithfully, by the time you get to the end of the game, it will be so hard that almost no one will be able to finish it. Think more about difficulty as a roller coaster. Each area the player goes through in the game will have its own curve where things slowly build up to a final confrontation, sometimes getting harder and occasionally allowing for a few minutes of breather but then ramping up again quickly, keeping the player alert and ready for the final challenge that will push his game-playing abilities to the limit.

The curve ultimately is all about how you've brought all the placement issues together to make the level: how much ammo you've provided, how many health and armor packs you've made available, how many and how densely the enemies are placed, and so on.

Always be your own harshest critic. Play through as you do initial placement passes. If you aren't having fun playing through your level, it's a good bet no one else will either. If things are feeling way too easy, limit the ammo available a little more or make those highly desirable health packs a little less available. Add a few extra gunners here or a sniper there to keep the player on his toes.

Alternatively, if it's too hard, thin out the enemy ranks a little bit. Add an extra checkpoint and maybe a few extra health packs at sensible spots. Your level is not going to be enjoyable if the player can't even make it 20 percent through. Being dead is no fun. Make it hard, but make it winnable.

Things to Avoid

Throughout this chapter, we've talked about things to do and things to avoid. Things to avoid warrants a little extra attention.

- **Always keep the game's limits in mind.** Just because you can place 42 roaming zombie cats in the level doesn't mean you should. Before you place something, first ask why it is there, and then ask yourself if this is the best place to do it.

- **Avoid arbitrarily overpowering the player.** If you want a sniper watching over a guard position, that's fine, but make sure the player can quickly take out the guard position and then figure out who the heck is firing at him. Making both aspects of that particular encounter really difficult is probably just going to result in a reload moment. Avoid encounters that encourage this kind of lazy gameplay.

- **Always think about what's fun.** You started down the path of level design because you love playing the games, presumably. While not everyone is going to agree on what's fun versus what isn't, you have to use your own prejudices initially to determine what is and what isn't. Then, once you have a playable level, start getting feedback on whether all those firefights you have to survive and computers you have to hack really add or subtract from the gameplay.

Example: Placing Units on Prospero's Island

Let's start getting into the details of placing objects in a game level. We'll continue using *Far Cry* for this part of the example. These examples are a little more tutorial oriented, but you should diverge from them as much as you want. This is just to give you the basic steps on placing things, while still thinking about the "why" of things, not yet "where" or "how."

We'll start with placing the boars, the zombies, and the big bad boss himself. Things to note before placing them are as follows:

- Our wild pigs are pretty low to the ground, so let's keep them on the beach. It's not very fair to the player to not have any sign that something is coming toward her. Of course there are reasons to have enemies in hard-to-see areas. If you're trying to create a higher degree of tension or a scare factor, having a tall wheat field in the middle of the night where zombies can pop out at any second can do a lot to scare the bejeebers out of the player. But we're not going for that, so they get to play in the sand, instead.

- As we move inland, the zombies have pretty much claimed all the tall grass areas and the volcano as their own, except of course for Mr. P's room at the top of the volcano. Start thinking about good places to plop some in the high grass —probably just wandering. A few should be guarding the entrance, possibly even a captain zombie. Place some in the rooms and probably a single zombie wandering the hallways. Make sure the entry to Prospero's room is guarded but that none are placed past there. He's the loner type.

- Prospero himself can be placed at the center of his pit of inequity, waiting to kill the players who dare to challenge him.

In addition, we need to think about other items we need to place. We aren't going to have vehicles, and there are no treasures to be found. So, we need weapons, ammo, health & armor packs, and possibly a key to get past the first room in the volcano.

Step 1: Placing the Player

Possibly the most important but easiest to overlook step that you need to make when laying out your level is giving your player somewhere to start! In *Far Cry*, these are respawn points. In multiplayer maps they define where you would actually respawn on death, but for our purposes, it's just giving the player a place to start. For larger levels, you'll want to consider multiple checkpoints/spawn points, but for our nice, tidy little level, one will do fine.

First off, move to the part of the island we're going to want to start in. In this case, the tip furthest from the volcano works. It's a small island, so no matter what, it'll be short.

Select the TagPoint button from your Objects toolbar, which will expose the various objects for that type. Our interest for now is just with respawn points, so select the "Respawn Point" option. As you move your mouse onto the landscape, you'll see a purplish-blue object with a yellow arrow on it. Place this as shown in Figure 6.4.

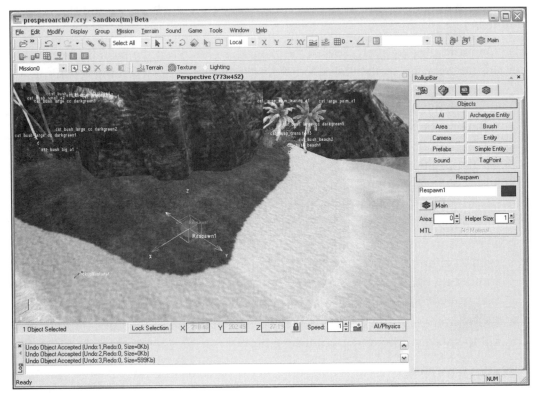

Figure 6.4 Respawn point placed.

You don't have to give it a specific name, but it is a good habit to get into, especially as levels get larger. For things as critical as respawn points, you want to be able to find them pretty quickly (see Figure 6.5).

Use a name that is appropriate but meaningful and not unnecessarily wordy. Choosing a naming convention can make it much easier to locate specific objects and actors. If this level of detail seems a little silly for this level, you're right. But when you're working on a level 20 times bigger with so much detail you can't remember half

Figure 6.5 Object naming and detail.

of it without looking, you'll be glad you started forming positive habits like this. Don't let these little sorting details get in the way of your creativity. Use them to encourage it. If you can track your complex ideas, they're that much easier to implement.

Step 2: Placing Enemies

Now that we can pop into the level, we need something to do there (see Figure 6.6). Let's start with some of the boars that the game has on the beach. Boars are a rather arbitrary decision, though fitting for a temperate island with a pretty closed ecosystem. If your intent is to make a much more fortified encampment, then choosing more zombies or guards would help with that.

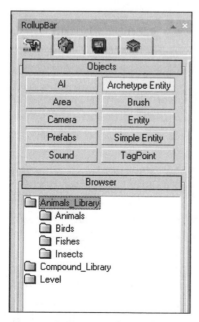

Select the Archeytpe Entity object button and drill down the list to Animals Library, Animals, Pig. Click and drag the Pig item onto the level. A little up the beach to the left of the spawn point will provide a good spot for its oinky goodness, close enough to be found quickly but, in case it's an angry pig, far enough to not rush the player instantly (see Figure 6.7).

As you can see, I've place two instead of just one. This gives a little more for the player to do, and two pigs are always better than one. Place a few more if you want; these pigs are not aggressive. But always err on the side of going a little light. It's always easy to go in and add a few more if you need to balance the difficulty.

Figure 6.6 Actor objects bar.

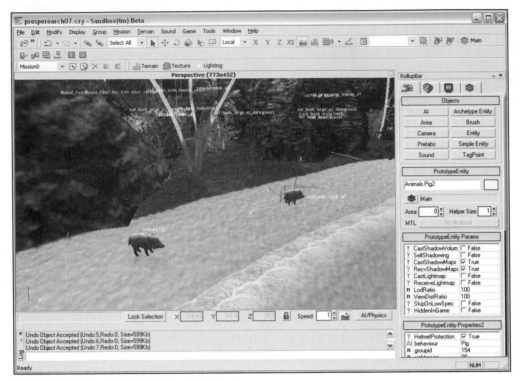

Figure 6.7 Boars placed and object detail.

Moving a little inland, we need to provide a few foes that actually inspire fear, so we introduce the zombie! In this case it's actually a mutant, but we'll pretend they're zombies (see Figure 6.8). They smell almost as bad.

Get to this in the same way as the pig. You'll find it under Archetype Entity, Compound Library, Mutant Fast. Place a couple on the interior island (the grassy regions). Think about placement. The zombies aren't overly bright, but maybe they are still smart enough to stay hidden initially (see Figure 6.9). Use some of the taller bushes, trees, and rocks to provide cover for them. Nothing provides a nice scare like going around a rock and getting your face bitten off by a partially decomposed ex-sailor.

Now that we have some stuff to fight on the intro part of the island, we need a few surprises in the corridors leading to Prospero and then the big man himself.

We're going to continue with two more of our speedy mutants inside. You may want a few more if these prove too easy, but they give us a good baseline. Place them as you like. On simple interiors, concealed corners or guarded doorways are always good initial choices. Think about ways you can challenge the player and make getting through an area more challenging than just "run in and shoot everything."

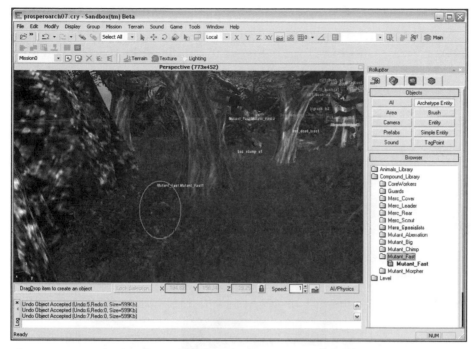

Figure 6.8 Zombies in the underbrush.

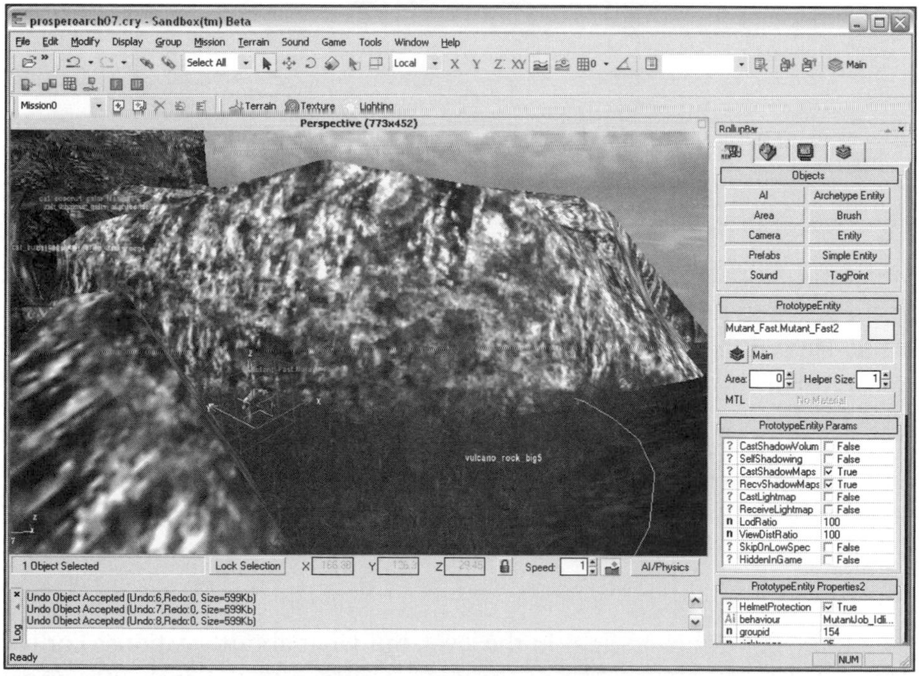

Figure 6.9 More hidden zombies.

I've added a few lights to the following scene (see Figure 6.10) to make things easier to see (refer back to Chapter 5 for more in-depth discussion of lighting and environmental effects), so please ignore the large lights in the middle of the space. If you want to place some of your own, the basic procedure to place them is the same as any object in *Far Cry*. Drag it onto the screen and place it where you want it.

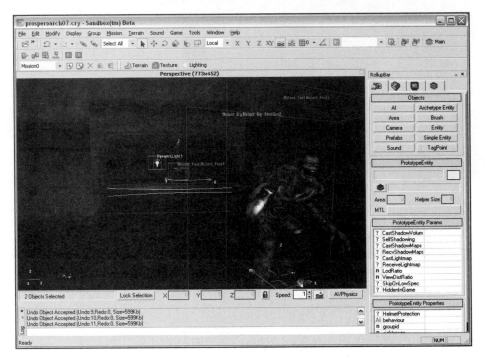

Figure 6.10 Interior of the volcano.

Finally, we need to place the "end boss" for our level—Prospero. We'll use the Big Mutant with the shotgun model. It can be found in the same object folder as our Fast Mutant zombie. He strikes a nice imposing figure and should visually let the player know he's in for a challenge (see Figure 6.11).

Place him up at the top of the volcano somewhere, a little way off from the elevator shaft. We want to make sure the player sees imminent death approaching before it actually unloads its guns.

Step 3: Phat Lewt

Now we have a bunch of things to fight in the level, but what about weapons? For the first part of the island, simply providing a machete should suffice. Let the player get up close and personal with a few enemies.

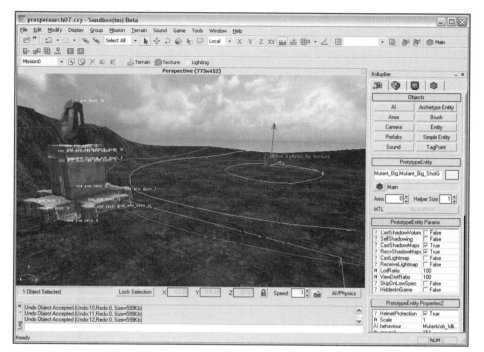

Figure 6.11 Top of the volcano.

You place weapons, armor, and health by going into Entity, Pickups and placing on the map what you want to provide, just like placing any other object or character (see Figure 6.12).

Now that the player has a machete, we'll want to think about prepping him for the final fights. In homage to all zombie movies, a shotgun seems fitting. When doing this, make sure you provide some shells, too (see Figure 6.13).

I decided to place these just inside the cave to provide some extra firepower for the final three fights. In addition to this, it's quite possible that the player has taken some damage at this point. We'll want to make sure the player doesn't go into those final fights on his last breath, so think about placing health and armor packs periodically if the player is likely to get into a lot of firefights (see Figure 6.14). Reloading from Save is not fun game design.

As for placement, that's a great start. You can always add more, tweak what you have, and get more creative with it, but thinking about your levels in terms of passes (first pass, second pass, final pass, and so on) is a great way to "layer" in content. Have fun with what you're doing. If you're having fun making your level, chances are that players will have fun playing your level.

Figure 6.12 Placing weapons.

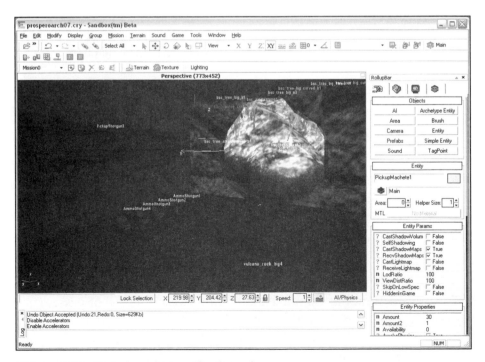

Figure 6.13 Shotgun and ammo for the end.

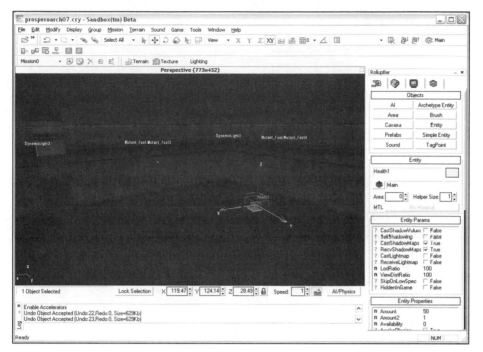

Figure 6.14 A med kit for the wounded.

What You Have Learned

We covered a pretty narrow topic in this chapter, but it is one that envelops so many elements of what makes a level a game. We talked about item placement, AI placement, and even a very specific type of trigger placement in the form of the respawn point.

Almost more important than any specific methods on how to do "things" in an editor though is an understanding of what you should and shouldn't do when designing your level. Placement is what most games come down to. The architecture and art style is important, but what you find while playing through those great environments is what keeps the player going.

Using those environments to make enemies harder to see, or seem like they're there for a reason, just adds to that realism. Combine that with the natural and, in some cases, extensible AI that most game actors have, and through the simple act of setting, that one actor in the ruined temple can change it from a scenic walk through to a fight for your life to get past him and to the lost codex of wisdom.

Review Questions

(Answers are located in Appendix C)

1. When choosing a spawn point for the player, what type of location would you look for?

    A. A location where the player can see and understand his first objective.

    B. A place where the player won't be immediately attacked.

    C. Both A and B

    D. None of the above.

2. Name a type of formation.

3. Why is spawning an enemy better than having him exist from the moment the level is loaded?

4. What is a spawn point?

5. What is bloodlocking?

6. What is an informational encounter?

On Your Own

1. Take the level you've been working on and add a player spawn point. Run the game and, from that spawn point, try to imagine what a first time player would think of what he sees. Have a friend run the game and ask him what his first impressions are. Will the player understand what he's supposed to do first, without having to read some in-game text or a cheat manual?

2. Place fifty moving non-aggressive entities within sight of the player's initial starting point. Start the game and see how slow your level runs. Adjust the amount of entities until you get an idea of the maximum number of entities you can have within sight of the player while still having good performance. Keep in mind, this will change depending on the machine, but it gives you a good baseline to work with. If you're on a high-end machine, turn the graphics settings way up. If you're on a lower-end machine, scale them back some.

3. Look at your level and think about what types of things you'd like to place to make it more interesting: Different or additional AI actors? A specific weapon type, or a few different weapons, but only a single clip of ammo for each? Play with it, alter it, add to it, or subtract from it. Keep playing it until your encounters feel "fun."

CHAPTER 7

BREATHING LIFE INTO YOUR LEVELS

So, you have this great level, and you've taken great care in placing every tiny little item, every powerup, every enemy. Unless you're lucky and have a game that comes with a super fun AI system for those default enemies, chances are, you still have a pretty boring game. Why? Because nothing is happening. Nothing moves, nothing talks. It really is the little things that come together to make a game feel alive.

Here's what you'll learn about in this chapter:

- Tools
- Pathing
- Triggers and traps
- Moving objects
- Conversation trees
- Objectives and quests
- Flags

Breath of Life

From talking NPCs to creatures wandering around to the ability to have an impact on the world you're playing in, it is those little things that help make the game real.

While there are many different techniques and things you can do to add life, this chapter will focus on some of the things that can add substance to your level.

Tools

The most common tools you'll find that assist you in the process of making your levels come alive are fortunately pretty consistent, at least in terms of how they look or the general knowledge base required to master them. Proprietary systems that are found in game studios usually share most, if not all, of these tools.

Scripting

If you decided that the path of game or level designer was what you really wanted to do, not only because of the inherent creative aspects but also because you can't program to save your life, that's okay. However, you absolutely must have some understanding of simple programming grammar and structure. These are *computer games*, after all. Every facet of your game is facilitated by lines and lines of computer code. Not having a basic knowledge of how to read and write this stuff can mean the difference between making a distinct, fun level or a drab, cookie-cutter level.

Another reason to know basic programming is that many game creation tools allow the level designer to make basic programs that grant him a great degree of power over how the game works. These small programs can do everything from changing how the AI works in a given situation, to determining how fast day and night go by, to altering the combat system so that the player's breath is a deadly weapon. These small programs are called "scripts."

Simply put, *scripting* is the interface through which the designer can actually change how stuff works in the game, determine new behaviors, or handle special interactions, such as triggers, locks, and anything else you can imagine (within the scope of what was exposed by the engine creator).

You lay out the levels with those art assets you've been provided, and you place actors that use both the developer's work through AI and the artist's work through look and animations, as well as all the goodies a commando in training could want.

Now you're stuck. You have no way to tell a specific actor that when the player crosses an invisible line in your level, he is to start pathing toward a specific target and then spout off some cool dialogue. This is where scripting can come in. Scripting can allow you to tie in seemingly unrelated actors in your level (NPCs, trigger regions, special effects, doors, elevators, traps, and even conversations) to create a cohesive, fun, and solid level for your players to then tear through.

For some games, like *Far Cry*, scripting can be as simple as setting up your level objectives, any special door or elevator behavior, and maybe a specialized trigger or two if the built-in system doesn't do what you want. For other games, such as *Neverwinter Nights*, scripting is a very critical aspect of how to affect a majority of the in-game behaviors, and how most events are handled.

Tip

Far Cry has an advantage in that the toolset, Sandbox Editor, can handle 99 percent of all events that need to be in the game. Trigger regions are defined clearly and easily through the use of standard geometric shapes, 2D, 3D, and a fairly powerful event/response system so that you can link, multilink, and react on most needed levels, including handling save points, objective changes, and so on.

This is somewhat advanced behavior and is covered extensively in the Sandbox FAQ and toolset documentation provided by CryTek. You should be aware of the system, and if you're terrified of programming, you can breathe a small sigh of relief if *Far Cry* is your chosen game engine to work in.

What You See Is What You Get

Many newer games, such as *Far Cry*, rely on WYSIWYG (What You See Is What You Get) systems to make the process of level building much easier and much more intuitive. While most of them also allow for use of scripting, it is not the only way to get things done, and often not the most efficient or easy. Other games, such as *Neverwinter Nights*, use a hybrid of WYSIWYG and scripting to provide a fairly powerful and customizable, but harder to master, environment.

In a WYSIWYG environment, many behaviors that you might normally tell the system how to do through scripting, you instead can do through a more natural "point and click" type interface. An area where this really makes your life easier is through pathing.

Example—Pathing in Neverwinter Nights

Say you want to move an individual from point A to point B in your game world. Without the use of a point and click system to "lay down" a path for your actor to follow, a system that only exposed it via scripting would require you to manually follow the path you want your actor to follow, making notes of the X,Y,Z coordinates at each stage, placing those in some type of data field, so that you could then feed it into a function that told the actor to walk to the various listed coordinates. Sound confusing? Well, it is. And if you're making a big game, with a lot of pathing actors, you can quickly see how much time you'd waste on a system like this.

```
pathdatatable = { (10, 3, 0),
                  (10, 7, 0),
                  (12, 9, 0),
                  (14, 11, 0) }

function somefunction( actor, pathdatatable )
    for k,v in pathdatatable do
            actor.gotopoint(pathdatatable[k])
            actor.waittilldone()
        end
end
```

While visually this doesn't look too horrible, imagine it repeated 1,000 times over the course of your game, presumably with paths much more complex than the simple four steps this one indicates.

Since it may not be obvious, let's step through what exactly this code is.

The line with "pathdatatable" is what its name would indicate, a table that contains the X, Y, and Z coordinates on some arbitrary map.

"somefunction" is just a random function that probably would do a lot more than this, but for now, just tells the "actor" to go to a certain point, inside a loop that assures that each item in our path table will get used. The "for k,v" section is a bit of LUA scripting syntax that makes it quick and easy to step through an entire table without generating a bunch of unnecessary steps or variables.

The last line of the "for k,v" loop just tells the actor to wait until it's done pathing to the first data point, so it can move onto the next one.

Well, that took longer than expected to explain, but that in itself is part of the problem. It's not nearly as fast to use a system like this for something most people think about in a very visual fashion.

Instead, let's look at how you can do this exact same thing in *Neverwinter Nights'* Aurora Editor.

Figure 7.1 shows a simple orc placed inside the *Neverwinter Nights'* toolset. If you were to right-click on the orc in the toolset, you would receive a menu that has a Create Waypoint option. The game automatically knows to assign this to the orc in question, and also links any additional waypoints you create. No need to manually go along the path, carefully notating your X, Y, and Z coordinates. Just point, click, move, and rotate so the path looks the way you want it to.

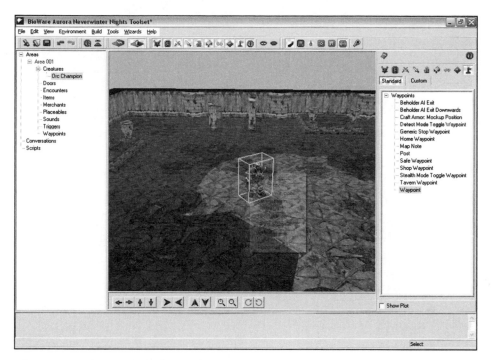

Figure 7.1 The Aurora toolset with an orc.

Check out Figure 7.2, and you can get a quick feel for what's involved. Going from Figure 7.1 to 7.2 was a simple matter of creating waypoints and moving them to where I wanted them. If I were to then load the game up, the orc would wander in that circle you see. That's really all there is to it, and many games have similar systems. *Far Cry* requires a little more care in the naming convention of the path objects, since they're not inherently tied to the actor in question, but this also allows for numerous actors to use the same paths.

Moving Objects

Movement can bring a level to life in a way that not much else can. It gives the player a feeling of being in a real world, with events going on around him. Pathing is one way to achieve this, but other forms of movement can come from vehicles and from other objects, such as lifts or elevators, a swinging light, or moving machinery in a room.

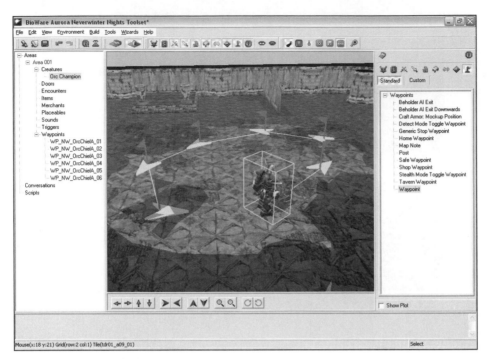

Figure 7.2 The orc with his path laid out.

Example: *Far Cry* Elevators

Some features, such as elevators (shown in Figure 7.3), were included as a built-in feature to the *Far Cry* toolset. Placing one is as simple as placing the object in question, and telling it what you want it to do and how fast you want it to move. If you load the sample *Far Cry* file for this chapter, you can see the elevator in action. Setting it up takes about five minutes. After you place and resize the object in *Far Cry*, you tell it what appearance you want it to have, and then tell it how high (or low) you want it to go, and how fast. Built-in features like this allow you to add seemingly complex behaviors to your map without having to understand physics or even scripting your own event/response behaviors to manage it.

From a player's perspective, a simple addition such as a lift can really add the feeling that the world they're playing in could be real. Not everyone uses stairs. Any tool is only as powerful as the uses you put it to. Learn your platform, and learn to exploit as much as you can. Your level will benefit from your pushing the bounds of what it, and you, can do.

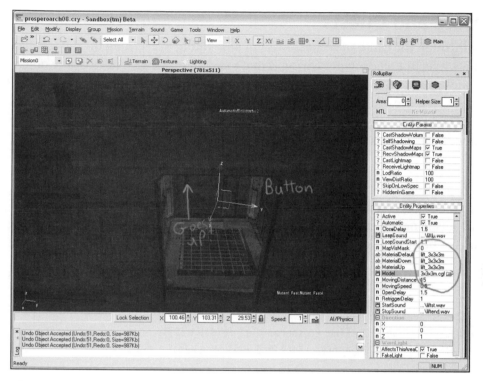

Figure 7.3 Prospero's Island's elevator.

Tip

Generally, built-in features like this are usually described in detail in the user manual for the toolset, and thankfully, that is the case with *Far Cry*. See page 51 of the Sandbox Editor User Manual for a step-by-step walkthrough of making an elevator in your level.

Moving Objects, Continued

Far Cry proves a better source of examples for moving objects, since it includes powerful, built-in methods for not only elevators, but also vehicles, including helicopters. To make a level feel really alive, seeing various enemies patrolling the bay in gun boats, or a sniper watching from his door in a helicopter that scours the land, gives you a lot of bang for your buck.

Objectives and Quests

Just going through the game in a linear fashion and killing everything on the way can be fun for a while, but tends to get boring if that's all you're doing. That's where objectives and quests come into play. In *Far Cry*, everything is an objective. Whether it's to infiltrate a secured area, kill an individual, or find a specific object, the objectives tell you what's next, and give you something to look forward to. In an RPG like *Neverwinter Nights*, quests are usually handled through conversations.

Examples: Scripting in *Far Cry*

Objectives in *Far Cry* use a combination of scripting and the WYSIWYG tools. This mixing of tools is not uncommon and, usually to create more powerful experiences, requires use of both to push your game platform as far as it can go.

The code aspects are pretty simple, and a common level might look something like this:

```
function Mission:Event_MainObjective()
        Hud:PushObjective({}, "Find Prospero. Kill Prospero!");
        Hud:AddMessage("New Objective: Find and kill Prospero", 15);
end

function Mission:Event_ObjectiveComplete()
        Hud:CompleteObjective("Find Prospero. Kill Prospero!");
        Hud:AddMessage("You killed Prospero! Oops. Now you're stuck here!", 120);
End
```

Now the code may seem a little obscure, but it's actually not doing too much. The first segment is the objective you'll want to give on entering the level, and the other segment is what you'll want to give once Prospero is retired. For a full listing of all the various commands available to you out the door, take a look at the Sandbox Editor User Manual.

The WYSIWYG aspects are also pretty straightforward to use, at least for *Far Cry*. The game uses trigger regions to handle most of its event/response behavior, and this type of behavior is no different (see Figure 7.4).

Far Cry has mini-wizards that allow you to quickly associate objects with other objects, and even scripts and functions in those scripts. This specific example is activated when the player enters the game, and it assigns the "Mission:Event_MainObjective()" to the player. Upon killing Prospero, he sends off an event to the game system that then provides the player with the "Mission:Event_ObjectiveComplete()" event.

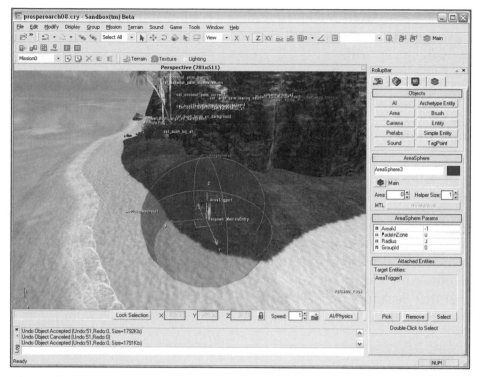

Figure 7.4 Entry trigger.

If you want to see this in action, load the Chapter 7 sample file for *Far Cry* into the editor and locate the blue sphere on the beach. Then press Ctrl+G to get into the quick game test mode and see if that works. When you pass through the area sphere, you'll see a small message appear on your hud, and if you press Tab, you'll see it listed on your objectives. Explore the level, take a look at the code and the various enemies placed on the level to see what events are associated with what. In this level, there are only two of note—the one you just looked at, and the "OnDeath" for Prospero to finish the level.

Examples: Quests in *Neverwinter Nights*

Quests in *Neverwinter Nights* are a little more abstract than the simple cause and effect objectives in *Far Cry*. They are made up of a series of flags, items, and conversations. Flags, as far as we're concerned here, are simply variables for tracking information, usually about a character in particular. These variables can be used to track whether an area has been explored, whether a specific NPC has been talked to, or whether a specific item has been found or destroyed. The interface for the players is usually as simple as a conversation with an NPC or reading a book that has some information in it. Some games include quest journals that you can use to allow the player to track their current assignments with.

The three main parts of a *Neverwinter Nights* quest are the conversation tree, the flags, and the item or NPC that is the objective.

Conversation Trees

Conversations are really the soul of how a game like *Neverwinter Nights* moves the story along. It is through conversations that the player gets history, finds out about heroic deeds that need to be accomplished, and gets rewarded for those deeds, other than just going out and slaying all the evil giant rats in the area.

Figure 7.5 shows a very simple conversation tree with an elven mage who is asking our hero if he would consider doing something for her. It uses a very easy tree format to present the conversation, where the top of each tree is the NPC's initial response, and anything after that depends on a combination of what responses the player gives, in addition to whatever flags the player has. Speaking of flags, that brings us to…

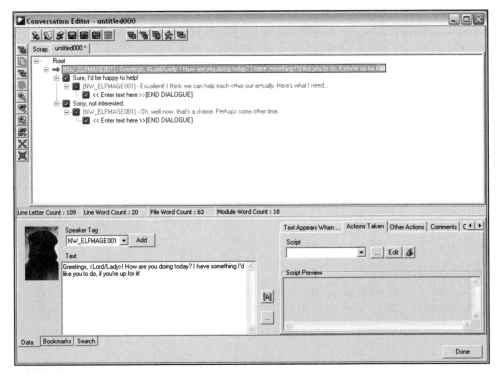

Figure 7.5 Basic conversation tree.

Flags

Flags are what ultimately control where the player is in his progress through your level, and how the computer tracks what information to make available to the player. Let's take a few minutes to look at how the conversation tree, the quest journal, and the script editor work together to provide something for the player to do, control what conversations are visible, and provide rewards.

The quest journal, as shown in Figure 7.6, is another even simpler tree view of information that allows you to create entries in the journal and provide "tags" or handles to each entry to refer to as needed to assign or take away.

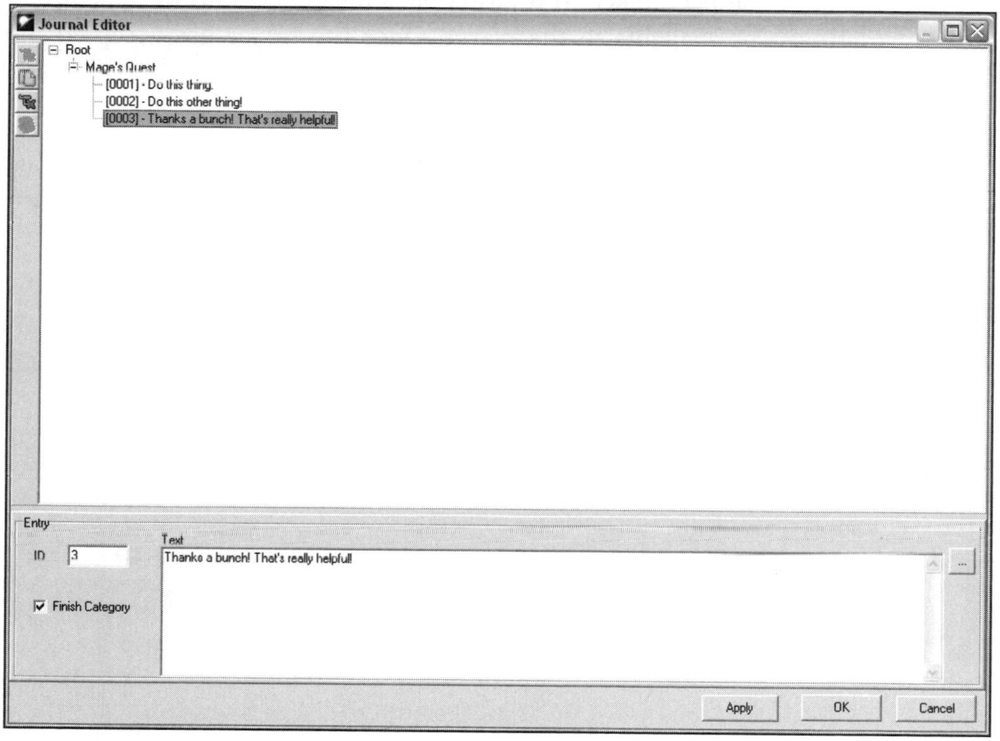

Figure 7.6 Quest journal.

In Figure 7.7, we see the interface that tells the game which part of the journal entry the player currently should see. But what do flags have to do with all this? Well, there are two things that flags are used for here. One, at various points in the conversation, we set certain local variables (our flags) to fairly simple values, such as:

```
int StartingConditional()
{

    // Inspect local variables
    if(!(GetLocalInt(GetPCSpeaker(), "nTakenQuest") == 1))
        return FALSE;


    return TRUE;
}
```

This is a very simple code snippet that checks for a flag called "nTakenQuest." It wants to know that the quest has been taken. If it hasn't been taken, this part of the conversation tree won't even be available to the player. Once the player has accepted the quest, it will be visible to him.

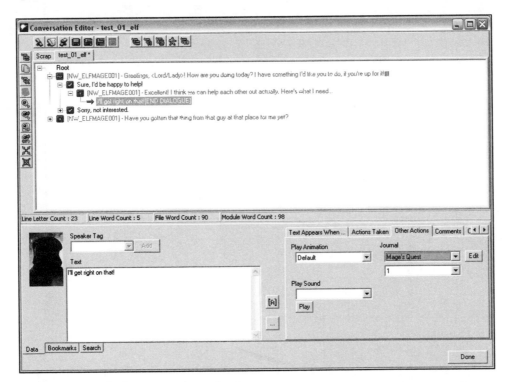

Figure 7.7 Assigning a quest journal entry.

Figure 7.8 is what *Neverwinter*'s script editor looks like. It's a very simple interface, with no extra bells and whistles, which is actually a good thing. It keeps it focused on what you're doing, without any of the extra confusion caused by a million random options available in a development environment like Microsoft's Visual Studio.

Figure 7.8 NWN's Script Editor.

In Figure 7.9, we see what a mostly finished conversation tree would look like, complete with the scripts it runs to check to determine what conversations to show. For a real level, hopefully your conversation would be a little better written than the quick dialogue I've thrown together for the purposes of this demo.

From a coding standpoint, a flag is nothing more than a variable getting set to a value then having that value tested at various points to determine what to do inside the game. With most games, using statements as simple as the last code sample shown can not only control quests and rewards in a conversation tree, but also determine if a specific actor will spawn (get generated by the game) into the world, whether the same actor can be found at an inn or at his house, or anything else within the scope of the game's abilities. Whatever your platform, learn how to use flags, and I strongly recommend getting comfortable with them quickly. They are a remarkably powerful tool.

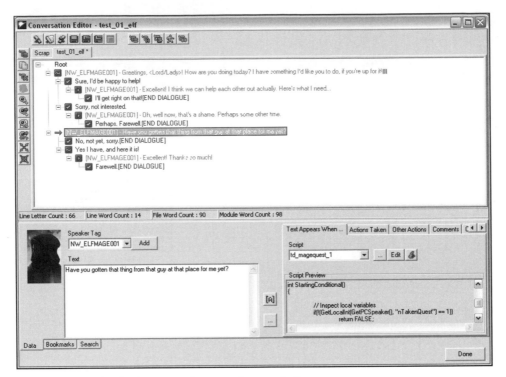

Figure 7.9 A finished conversation tree, flags and all.

Tip

For an in-depth tutorial on the basics of the *Neverwinter Nights'* Aurora toolset, go to http://nwn.bioware.com/builders/pdf/AuroraToolsetTutorial.pdf. In addition, http://nwvault.ign.com is also one of the most widely used resources available for world builders using *Neverwinter Nights* as their platform.

A More Advanced Script

Just so you can see what occurs in a more complex design, I've included the following standalone script. Spend some time analyzing it, and determine what's going on. Being able to read and at least decipher what is going on in a script or piece of code is a very valuable skill for a designer, and being able to write the code yourself can sometimes save you a lot of time and effort if you tried to do the same task through some other mechanism.

I've left in a few major function comments but removed anything that clearly spelled out what a specific line of script was doing.

This script is from a massively multi-player game that was cancelled in early 2004. The code shown is the first few functions for a level that had a very large scale battle occurring in it.

```lua
-- ** Load needed libraries here
dofile("..\\Assets\\AIScripts\\core.lua")
dofile("..\\Assets\\AIScripts\\utils.lua")
LoadLocalLibrary("midgard", "MID5_HUM_PassDef", "constants.lua")


-- ****************************************
-- ** EnteredZone is used to get everything going. All setup should be
performed here, including the timer to
-- ** auto start the war, if we go that route.
-- ****************************************
function EnteredZone(player)
    print("Entered Zone function...")

    if ( g_RunOnce == false ) then
        ge_Wave1Started = ReflexUserEvent( "w1sn" )
        SpawnStandardGroup( "Mid5_TheCavalry", "MID5_HUM_TheCavalry", 1)
        SpawnStandardGroup( "Mid5_ThomsIronFist", "MID5_HUM_ThomsIF", 1)
        SpawnStandardGroup( "Mid5_JaisBowmen", "MID5_HUM_JaisBowmen", 1)
        SpawnStandardGroup( "Mid5_KyansBrigade", "MID5_HUM_KyansBrigade", 1)
        SpawnStandardGroup( "Mid5_CarsonsBerserkers", "MID5_HUM_CarsonsBerskrzs", 1)
        Mid5_PickLocations()
    end

    for k,v in Players do
        if ( type(v) == "table" ) then
            ShowUI(v)
        end
    end


    local m5grp1 = ReflexTimerEvent( "mgr1", EFT_Always, 15.0, Mid5_MakeGroups )
end

-- ************************
-- ** War Tracking
-- **
-- ** This is used to track the war.
-- ** Depending on the wave, a number of different things
-- ** are run, including checking which targets should be considered.
```

```
-- ***********************
function Mid5_DogOfWar(me)
    local DogLoop = ReflexTimerEvent("M5Tent1", EFT_Always, 5.0)
    me:SetAIProperty( WanderRadius, 0 )
    me:SetAIProperty( AggroDistancePercent, 0.0 )

    while ( g_Zero == 0 ) do
        if ( g_HCT_Destroyed == true ) and ( g_HCB_Destroyed == true ) and (
g_HCA_Destroyed == true ) then
                g_HC_Destroyed = true
        end

        if (g_CurrentWave == 1) then
            Wave1Running()
        end

        if (g_CurrentWave == 2) then
            Wave2Running()
        end

        if (g_CurrentWave == 3) then
            Wave3Running()
        end

        WaitForEvent( DogLoop )
    end

end
```

So for a quick run down of what's occurring in each function:

> The first three lines are a fairly common sight in any program and even most scripts. They're script files that have been designed to collect common tools and functions in one place to provide the designer frequently needed functionality without needing to write the code himself.

> The first function, "EnteredZone," is run once, upon the player(s) entering the level. It spawns all the needed actors for the war to occur, determines all the players that entered the level, and sets a 15-second timer that will call another function to get things going. A couple second wait in scripts is a common way to make sure other needed scripts or objects have fully loaded into a level before continuing.

The final function, "Mid5_DogOfWar," is a never-ending loop set on an actual entity in the level—our "Dogs of War," if you will. The actor is set to be invisible and invincible elsewhere, but the second and third line also tell him to not move at all, and to never attack anyone. He's just there to count. The big "While/Do" loop that makes up the rest of the function just checks a global variable (flag) for its state and runs a function elsewhere in the script to check for other events and to trigger other actions.

This script was written in Lua, in case the syntax looks a little strange for anyone used to C, C++, or Java. If you would like to see the full script from which this segment was pulled, check out: http://www.nwdragon.com/mid5.htm.

Other Forms of Life

There are many different ways you can make your levels feel more alive. In addition to the various ways already discussed, consider the following methods to add that little something extra:

- Environmental sound effects
- Particle systems to emulate insect swarms, steam vents, etc.
- Music appropriate to the levels theme
- Cutscenes to advance the story and allow for scripted events
- NPC to NPC interactions (Meeting in the streets, discussing NPC Y's orders for the day, etc)

There are many more things you can do, and a lot of it depends on the game in question. Explore the possibilities, and never forget that the little things can go a long way to make your levels feel like a real world.

What You Have Learned

In this chapter, we've seen how two specific games handle tasks, from making an elevator, to giving objectives, to building fairly complex conversation trees. The topics in this chapter alone are the subjects of entire books, Web sites, and tutorials. In addition to the resources already listed as we've gone through this chapter, consider looking into the following books/guides:

- *Game Programming with Python, Lua, and Ruby* by Tom Gutschmidt (Premier Press, 2004)
- *Versus Books Official Neverwinter Nights World Builder's Perfect Guide* by Casey Loe, Versus Staff, Patrick Cunningham (Versus Books, 2004)

■ *Character Development and Storytelling for Games* by Lee Sheldon (Course PTR, 2004)

Review Questions

(Answers can be found in Appendix C)

1. What is a script?
2. What types of things can a script control?
3. When building a quest for a game, what elements can you expect to have to plan for/implement?
4. What types of objects, moving or otherwise, could you add to an abandoned military base to give it more life and flavor?

On Your Own

Build a fully flushed out quest in your game. If supported, it should be started and finished by a conversation, either with an actor appropriate to the setting, or through an object (a scroll, a computer, a mystical orb of Fnarg).

The quest should have at least three steps along the way, and involve at least a few of the following:

■ A foe to be defeated
■ Something that needs to be found, either of the foe, or hidden away somewhere
■ Conversing with another actor to get more information
■ Breaking into a locked house/chest/tomb
■ Exploring a location
■ Defeating numerous (or a specific number of) foes
■ Provide a cool reward

Most of all, make it fun, interesting, and a way to advance your level, not just as busy work for the player. Think of a cool story to attach to it, a cool item that the player will get as a reward, and how it will fit in with your overall design.

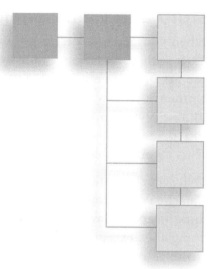

CHAPTER 8

DIALOGUE
AND STORY

There is much argument these days on the role of story in modern games. Some people think story is really only an afterthought, tacked on as an excuse for a setting. Others claim it is the reason for modern games, the essence of what gamers want in their hobby.

In this chapter, we'll discuss the role of story in games and take a look at how to make stories for games.

In this chapter, you'll learn the following:

- How story is used in games
- Why story for games is different from story in other media
- What typcs of stories work with what types of games
- How to create great characters
- How to create great plots
- How to write dialogue
- About voicelines and how they're used in games
- How to write good dialogue for in-game messages and cutscenes
- About conversation trees and how to create them

Story and Game: Enemies and Allies

When you begin to design a game, it usually starts with a story. Actually, it usually starts with a scene. You're thinking about what kind of game you'd like to make, and you get a picture in your head of a scene from your game, a "Wouldn't it be cool if…" moment that gives you a rush of inspiration. Perhaps it's a scene where you play a zombie trying to defeat well-armed redheads, or a fast-paced space shooter where you're dodging laser blasts while trying to smuggle a load of valuable Antares Lion's Tears through a blockade of Galactic Police.

That scene expands into a story by its own accord. You begin to ask yourself why the Galactic Police would want to stop the smuggling of Lion's Tears? Maybe there's something deeper. Maybe the smuggler (the player) would normally have no problem doing this, except that he's stumbled onto a galactic war! Maybe the shipment of Lion's Tears isn't really Lion's Tears, but the daughter of the Galactic Emperor (let's call her Gretchen) in a box labeled "Lion's Tears—not really a stowaway princess!" Maybe….

Well, you get the point. Suddenly, there is story. Next, if you're lucky, you write the thing down, you hash it out with your team, you get everybody excited, somebody gives you money to build it, and three years later, it's a game! It's on the shelves, the first reviews come in and….

No one mentions Gretchen. No one seemed to have figured out that Count Stephan was, in fact, controlling the forces on Fingus 5. Large amounts of important detail were passed by completely as people rushed to get the plasma saber and cut their way through legions of NPCs, without listening to the cool voicelines that you spent nearly a quarter of your budget on, thus not being able to spend as much on the graphics, which is why your game shows up as a painful 6.8 on Gamerankings.com.

In short: No one cares about your darn story!

No one except those embarrassing fanatics who insist on writing fan fiction about the love trysts between Gretchen and the evil Slug Lord of Orion 6, but we're not counting them.

"This is impossible!" you think. Story is what makes us human. In his book *Story*, Robert McKee says "Our appetite for story is a reflection of the profound need to grasp the pattern of living…" How can story not be important to these people? Obviously, my friend, you're living on the planet with a bunch of Neanderthals.

Or maybe not.

Has this ever happened to you? You're driving to a new place in a city. You're looking at street sign after street sign, trying to find your way to the store or a friend's house or wherever you're going. You pass by unfamiliar buildings. You drive past a road with no street sign. "Was that the one?" you think. It probably wasn't, but you feel worry boiling up in your stomach. Unconsciously, your hand reaches out, and you turn off the radio.

Why? Why did you just turn off the radio? Because it was a distraction, even though you weren't even listening to it in the first place. It was enough of a drag on your mental processes that you needed to turn it off.

Turning Off the Radio

Games put you in similar circumstances to driving in an unknown environment. Especially in action-oriented, story-driven games, the player is thrust into one new environment after another. He's expected to do complicated maneuvers involving combinations of buttons that he can't look at, in fear of not seeing some sort of sudden attack. He's supposed to discern enemy from friend from odd-looking piece of static environment using a camera that seems to get stuck in the worst places imaginable.

Under these circumstances, is it any wonder that the player has no patience for story? Is it surprising that subtlety of any type completely bypasses him like a malfunctioning Sidewinder missile?

In 1943, psychologist Abraham Maslow wrote a paper called, "A Theory of Human Motivation," which was then expanded into a book in 1954 called, *Motivation and Personality*. In these writings, Maslow explored what he called a human hierarchy of needs.

The hierarchy of needs is a pyramid of goals, each one having to be fulfilled before the next can be obtained (see Figure 8.1). There are five levels: physiological needs, safety needs, love and belonging needs, esteem needs, and self-actualization needs.

What this means is that a human needs to satisfy his physiological goals (food, water, and air) before he can start looking for safety (shelter and warmth), which he needs to satisfy before he can start looking for love and acceptance and so on. If you'll notice, aesthetic needs are pretty far up the list.

Players follow a similar hierarchy (see Figure 8.2).

1. They must first understand the interface of the game. Without knowing what buttons to push or how to control the game, the player has no mental capacity for the story.

2. Then, he has to feel safe. If the player finds himself in a situation that calls for action, or if he finds himself fearful about what's going to leap out at him next, the player probably has no time to understand the story.

3. Then he has to understand the goal. A player probably feels the need to know his immediate goal before he'll pay attention to your story. Though the goal might come to him in the midst of a story element, perhaps through a text message, he'll probably skip most everything until he gets to what he's supposed to be doing. Remember, the player doesn't like to be confused.

4. Finally, after all that is accomplished, the player can start looking for subtleties such as the story and Easter eggs and sub-quests if he wants to search. Some never get past stage 2.

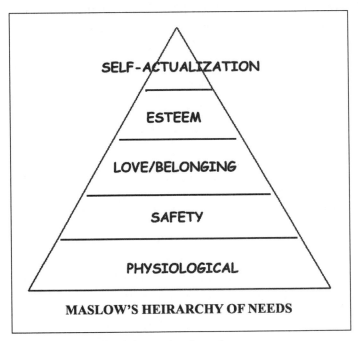

Figure 8.1 Maslow's hierarchy of needs.

With this in mind, it's pretty easy to see why the story can be so easily ignored. The player has a lot to worry about before he can pay attention to a text pop-up telling him the long and involved story of how Princess Gretchen's uncle's barber had seen the perfect hair style on a woman he once passed on the way to his favorite kosher deli.

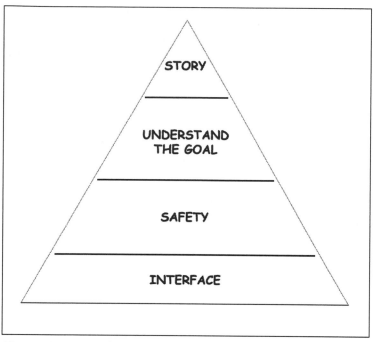

Figure 8.2 Hierarchy of player needs.

Shoving Story into the Game

Now that I've discouraged you, it's time to talk about how to fix this problem. The point I've been trying to make is that you have to be clever in trying to deliver story content. Just treating a game like it is a novel or a movie isn't the way to go, because even the most straightforward game is both interactive and non-linear, which novels and movies aren't. The player isn't a captive who has to follow your game step by step just the way you planned it. No, the player will happily pass by anything he can skip, do things backward, from the inside out, or any which way that captures his interest at that moment.

Basically, telling stories in games is different from telling stories in linear media.

Not all is lost, however. You have one very strong ally on your side: the player himself. As mentioned in the Robert McKee quotation previously, story is the framework in which we all live. People yearn for stories in games. I can't tell you how many times I've heard a game reviewer or forum post complain that there isn't enough story in games these days. There is a definite demand for it.

The player wants a story. You want to tell a story. The medium in which you want to tell the story causes a huge disconnect. What do you do?

Lowering the Bar

The first thing you might want to do is create a game that has a simple interface, little or no twitch-style action, and immediately identifiable goals. If you lower the bar on the hierarchy, the user will find it easier to soak in your story. In other words, create an adventure game.

Adventure games have very simple interfaces, usually of the point-and-click variety. They rarely have any action elements in them. (And when they do, they usually get hammered for including them.) The mission and the storyline usually are inextricably intertwined such that players have to sit through 90 percent story to find the 10 percent knowledge they need to understand and act on the mission requirements.

However, adventure games aren't that popular anymore. Adventure games are intensely frustrating at times and usually end up making the player feel stupid. Both aspects present big problems that cause people's trigger fingers to get itchy for something a bit more brutal.

Alternating Content

Another thing you can do is alternate storytelling and action. You artificially erase the lower hierarchy needs by removing all control from the player and shove some story on him. Gameplay like this is exemplified in roleplaying games of the Japanese variety, particularly games such as Square/Enix's *Final Fantasy* series, but it is basically the standard method of storytelling in most games in one way or another.

In these games, the story is told in a series of cutscenes interspersed with periods of action. The player is frozen out of the game while a miniature movie plays. Sinister plots are revealed; conversations between the player's avatar and those he meets take place; and other bits of story happen in these miniature movies. When this is finished, the player is then allowed control over the game.

As has been covered in this book, the problem with this is that, by taking control away from the player, you're disrupting the player's immersion, which can be frustrating. Also, if the player enters an unfortunate loop of seeing the cutscene, dying, and then being forced to watch the (hopefully skippable) cutscene all over again, the frustration level grows higher. However, many games use this tactic successfully, as players have now become accustomed to this style of storytelling.

The secret of successfully alternating story and game lies in establishing a predictable pattern of where and when the player can expect to find those cutscenes. In many games, cutscenes happen between levels when the player accomplishes his goal, moving the plot a bit further by pretty much explaining to the player the implications of what he's just done (for example, escaped from the Deathstar with the secret plans) and what he needs to do next (go back and destroy the thing).

Puzzle Pieces

Dispersing information like puzzle pieces is also a way to bring story to the player. In this method, the player has a chance to interact with storytelling nodes throughout the game. These nodes can be things such as friendly NPCs wandering about, newspapers the player can pick up and read, or text bulletins that appear in the player's interface.

This is an interesting way to tell a story, but it's totally nonlinear. Since you can't count on the player to pick up the story bits in any particular order or read them at all, you'll need to be clever if you want any information whatsoever to get into the player's head.

Because of this, this type of storytelling usually is used with one of the other story methods. The player might learn something by talking to an NPC or reading a story, but the game designer, not being able to trust the player to pay attention to them, gives out the important stuff in a cutscene later.

The Ever-Present Companion

In Naughty Dog's game *Jak and Daxter*, the faithful sidekick Daxter accompanies the hero, Jak, as they work their way jumping and climbing through the game. This type of arrangement gives the designer an excellent way to impart story to the player, as the ever-present companion helps to narrate the story as action takes place.

The bad side to this is that the companion needs to be fun to have around instead of frustrating. In *Jak and Daxter*, Daxter rides on Jak's shoulder as if Jak has a second head. Sometimes Daxter is even used as a weapon! But usually Daxter maintains almost zero impact on the action, while giving the designers a chance to impart information and clues seamlessly within the framework of the game.

In other games, the sidekick becomes an important part of the gameplay as a helper to the player's cause. The bad side of this is that unless this is done really well, the player has to continually shepherd the sidekick to make sure he isn't in trouble. Developing this is also a nightmare in terms of balancing and AI pathing. This is why you see a lot of talking heads on computer screens and hear magic voices in games these days. They can be ever present and cause the developers much less of a headache.

Finally, another type of ever-present companion is the player's avatar. In the form of "talking to himself," the avatar tells the story as a form of first-person narration. Once again, this is good for the developers but can be jarring for the player. By using this method, you're essentially putting words in the player's mouth.

Other Methods of Relating Story

There are many ways to tell a story, whether within games or elsewhere. Because of the human need to shape stories around all that they perceive, the way to tell those stories is as infinite as the imagination.

One of the best ways of communication, and thus storytelling, is through the human face and body. Body language and facial expressions are dense with understandable information for us. Having NPCs smile, frown, laugh, put their hands on their hips, or shake their fists gives the player a lot of information about that NPC. One recent game that did a good job with body language was Sony's *ICO*. In this game, the hero, a young boy with horns, tries to save a little girl while working to escape a creepy castle filled with shadows that come to life. Hardly a word is spoken, but the player can instantly sense the relationship between the boy and the girl by the way the boy has to hold her hand when they move. In a moment, the developers have told us a story that would have taken many words of explanation in a text screen.

This method has its faults, though. A person's interpretation of body language and other signs is highly individual and usually based on culture. You can't determine with a high degree of accuracy that the message you're trying to send is the one players will receive.

Writing Story for Games

Writing a story for games, as we have covered, is not the same as writing for movies or novels. Because of the interactive and non-linear nature of games, the skills you learn from English and creative writing and screenwriting classes don't have as much relevance as they do for more linear media. However, this is not to say that those lessons are useless for games. They're just not as transmittable as some people think.

Game Stories Are Character Based

Because of the their non-linear nature, games rely more on characters and what they can tell players than on written text or disembodied narration. In games, non-player characters become information nodes, dispensing clues and plot points as the player bounces from one to another like a pinball. Having rich, deep NPCs is essential to creating a personality for your game. Think about a game you've played that you felt had a great story. See if you can picture and name the characters in that game that were your favorites.

Next, think about a game you didn't think had a good story. Are the characters in that game memorable at all? If they are, do you remember them fondly, or do you remember them out of irritation?

If you're like me, you probably can remember at least some of the names and all the faces of the characters in the good story game. Those characters are a big reason you thought the story was so good.

To understand how to make great characters, I once again refer to Robert McKee's excellent book, *Story*. In it, McKee talks about the difference between character and characteristics.

Characteristics are observable qualities: how a person looks, his likes and dislikes, his favorite color, the way he likes his toast, and so on.

Character, according to McKee, can be expressed only through the choices a character makes under pressure: the way the character reacts in a moral dilemma, for example, or what he does when a bomb goes off nearby.

When creating the characters for your game, it will be easy to come up with characteristics. A peasant dresses in brownish clothing and has a bowl haircut. A tough mercenary carries a big gun and chomps down on a cigar. Creating character, though, is fiendishly hard. It takes serious scripting and AI to make character work in real time as you determine how a character will react to any one of a dozen possible circumstances.

However, if you want a good story in your game, you'll have to work hard to do just that. The following are some tips on building good characters:

- Show, rather than tell, the player your character's reactions to stressful events. Make him angry; make him scared; have him care for the player. Put him in moral quandaries.

- Love your characters. Over-design them. Give them histories that the player will never see and try to suggest those histories through the character's reactions.

- Get good voice talent. A good actor will make a character come alive.

- Make your characters as human as possible. To understand characters, a player needs to be able to relate to them. Give them understandable qualities.

- All of your character's actions should have consequences. From the biggest to the smallest, if a character does something, try to make that something matter in some way.

- Your characters should have both strengths and flaws. Flaws make characters human.

The Player Character

One of the main differences between games and movies or novels is that the main character in a game is the character you probably want to spend the least amount of time developing.

The player, by and large, will determine the nature of his avatar through his own actions. He'll decide how he responds to danger and moral choices that occur during gameplay. If you force a decision or reaction on the player, you'll risk alienating him.

For instance, you want the player to be the "good guy." During a cutscene that features the player, he is given the choice between saving his best friend from certain doom and running after the main villain and shooting him in the head. In your cutscene, you make the decision for the player: He goes to save his friend. However, the player might not want that. Maybe he doesn't care a whit about his friend; he just wants to kill that creep who put him in this dilemma. By forcing the player's hand, you've alienated him. He now thinks of his avatar as a weenie that can't make the tough decisions.

To keep this from happening, always try to give the opportunity to make the choice when you present him with a problem. A good example of a game that does this is *Fable* by developer Big Blue Box Games. The main character is continually given the choice to do whatever he feels is appropriate in whatever circumstance he finds himself in.

The Villains

Your villains should be some of the best-developed characters in your game. Nothing is worse than finding yourself up against the final boss and finding you don't care about beating him.

Villains require development. You can't just pop them into the end without reminding the player about their presence once in a while. You should expose the player to them at intervals through the story, through either other characters talking about him or actual appearances.

The villain should grow alongside the player. As the player meets the villain, more and more character is revealed as the player's actions affect the villain's plans. You need to somehow show those reactions through changes in the villain's plans or method of operation.

A villain the player can empathize with is better than one he finds totally alien. It's always nice to have the evil guy who indiscriminately kills at a whim, but a villain who thinks he is acting for the greater good is more interesting. Also, show the villain's human side. Show him when he's not quite prepared to deliver his evil speeches. Show him when he gets angry or when he's disappointed. Show him making decisions.

Many times, a villain shows his evil to the player through the things he does to other characters in the game, such as taking hostages or killing loved ones. This won't provide motivation for the player unless he has had enough exposure to the victim to develop feelings for that victim. A villain's potency is increased when other characters in the game are also fully developed.

Thoughts on Plot

The plot is the story of your game. It's created through a series of events, which take the player from the beginning of your game to the end.

The plot, on a macro level, is pretty much the same as the kind of plots you find in movies and novels. You have a beginning, a middle, and an end. Inside those areas (where we find the non-sequential nature of the events as the player chooses how he goes about playing the game) is where games diverge from other storytelling media. But in a large sense, it all comes out much the same.

In most cases, game plots are pretty cut and dried, some might even say cliché. The hero is always fighting against impossible odds as the fate of the world hangs in the balance.

One of the reasons for this is that games revolve mostly around adventure. Adventure is an action-oriented story type, where the main character strives to bring about a successful conclusion. Unfortunately, while adventures have a lot of scope in terms of what you can do with them, they all seem a little formulaic after a while.

Not that this is all bad. If clichéd stories do one thing well, it is make the player feel right at home. Clichés have a lot of information packed into them, because people know what to expect from them. Mention something like "Holy Grail," and a myriad of King Arthur, his Round Table, Lancelot, Sir Gawain, and possibly Indiana Jones images pop into people's minds. Set a player as a smuggler trying to get Lion's Tears past the Galactic Police, and the player will instantly know what his place is in your universe and what to expect (in general) from your game.

The danger of using clichés, however, is that you risk boring the player. Luckily, the answer to making even the worst clichés work is good characters. So, while you can make your plot cliché, never do the same to your characters.

Creating a Good Plot

All stories have a *who, when, where, what, why,* and *how.* The *who* is the characters. The *when* and the *where* make up the setting. The *what, why,* and *how* give us the plot.

We have some characters, and they exist somewhere in time. But they need to do more than exist. They need to have a purpose, a motivation for getting from the beginning of the story to the end (just as an audience or game player needs to have a reason to proceed through your adventure).

What

Imagine you're reading a book or watching a movie about a scientist who works in a lab. As the story opens, we see him get up in the morning, eat breakfast, shower, brush his teeth, shave, get dressed, go to work, work for four hours, take a break for lunch, work for another four hours, leave work, drive home, make dinner, eat dinner, watch the news, read a book, brush his teeth, put on his pajamas, and go to sleep. The next morning he gets up, eats breakfast, showers, brushes his teeth, shaves, gets dressed, goes to work, and so on. It wouldn't be long before you flung the book across the room or stomped out of the theatre and demanded your money back. The reason is that nothing is happening in the story. There's plenty of movement, but there's nothing worth watching.

Now let's imagine that our scientist works for a lab in a top-secret military facility. At least now we know our guy isn't a total dolt. He's got a very important job in a place where they probably screen the applicants pretty well before they hire them. Still, he hasn't yet done anything to pique our interest. OK, let's flesh him out some more. He works in a top-secret military facility, which is developing an alternative source of fuel. Success would mean that the world would not be dependent on fossil fuels for heat and transportation. Great! There's just one problem.

Why

There are a lot of factions who would not want to see that happen. They have too much invested in keeping the world dependent on oil and gas. If word of what our hero was up to got out, there are those who would go to any lengths to disrupt the project and destroy his work.

If word *didn't* leak out about our scientist's efforts, we would be back to the same book we tossed earlier, because he would get up and go to work every day and eventually complete his project successfully and that would be that. Our story needs to have his secret get out. Why is he working on this project? Presumably, to help the world have more options. Why would people want to stop him? Perhaps they own oil companies. Perhaps they fear the alternatives. Perhaps they just don't like our hero and want him to fail. Whatever the reason, they have found out what he is doing, and they intend to interfere.

How

How will they keep him from fulfilling his goal? How will he and the agency he works for prevail? What will become of our scientist? What will become of his enemies? All of these questions make up the *how* of our story. How will it end? I don't know yet. But at least now there is a story, whereas before there was meaningless action. What we have done is create a *conflict* that, hopefully, our audience will care about and become immersed in enough to finish our book, watch our movie, or play our game.

Where Do Plots Come From?

It is likely that you're presented with several potential plots every day. You just have to know where to look for them.

One obvious source is the news. Whether you read the newspaper, watch a newscast, or get your news online, the things that happen to real people in real life are rich fodder for fictitious plots. It is said that truth is stranger than fiction, but you can find material in almost any news piece you see.

Sometimes all it takes is catching a quick glimpse of something. Some small, almost unnoticed action grabs your attention and holds it just long enough for your mind to start constructing a before and after.

Another method for finding potential plots is examining the values you hold and comparing them to their opposites. For example, if you're a strict vegetarian, you might wonder how anyone could eat meat, wear leather, or use animal products in medicines. If it is the goal of the characters in your game to get from Point A to Point B, no matter how they have to do it, then it is guaranteed that they are going to meet other characters that want to stop them. Maybe they oppose the method your characters used to get there, such as killing elephants to use their tusks as canoe paddles.

That opposition will be where you find your gameplay. Your plot becomes a framework of story in which the friction between the player and his adversaries is played out in the mechanics of your game.

It's been said that all songs are about one of three things: The guy meets the girl, the guy gets the girl, or the guy loses the girl. It's also been said that all stories are basically about the struggle between good and evil. If these assumptions are true, then it's your job as a game designer to find an innovative way to make the plot of your game uniquely yours. You don't have to come up with a never-before-told story. You just have to put your spin on the plot.

Dialogue

Conversations between characters deliver the bulk of the story in many games. What a character says to another can reveal his inner nature, give the player clues as to where to go next, or even provide gameplay.

Dialogue is usually delivered in games through the use of *voicelines*. Voicelines are individual sound files that contain one individual thought or phrase, usually not longer than a paragraph.

For example, let's look at the following conversation:

Player: "Why are you here? Why are you stuck in this box labeled 'Lion's Tears—not really a stowaway princess?' Don't you know enough to at least get in a box labeled 'Princess, Handle with Care?'"

Princess Gretchen: "I had to escape! My father had betrothed me to the evil Slug Lord of Orion 6 and left me no choice but to flee to the stars in this wretched box with my faithful robot companion Saturn-13 and my dog Biscuit!"

If this conversation were turned into voicelines, it might look like this:

Why are you here?

Why are you stuck in this box labeled "Lion's Tears—not really a stowaway princess"? Don't you know enough to at least get in a box labeled "Princess, Handle with Care"?

I had to escape!

My father had betrothed me to the evil Slug Lord of Orion 6 and left me no choice but to flee to the stars in this wretched box with my faithful robot companion Saturn-13 and my dog Biscuit!

Whenever a good pause occurs, a new voiceline is generated. Sometimes the pause between sentences is great enough to break up a paragraph, and sometimes it isn't. It's usually up to whoever is recording the audio to make those decisions.

In some games, such as sports games, voicelines are broken up even more. A line such as "It's first down on the ten yard line with nine minutes to go in the second quarter" might be constructed using several voicelines because the game is designed to be modular to save on how many voicelines it uses. Instead of having a separate voiceline for each possible first down on any yard line at any time in any quarter, the sentence is broken up something like this:

<It's first down on the> <ten> <yard line with> <nine> <minutes to go in the> <second quarter>

This type of division is very hard to do. Splicing sentences out of individual words is extremely hard, even for professionals with modern equipment. However, when you have the choice between this and having to record an almost infinite number of voice-lines, you begin to think that having a weird-sounding sentence here and there might not be so bad after all.

Writing Dialogue

Writing dialogue is a bit different in games from what it is in most other media. This is due to the short attention span of the player, whose patience for dialogue is limited because his reflexes have been ramped up by the action of the game. In fact, for dialogue uttered within the action of a game, such as someone calling the player over a radio, it's best to keep your voicelines pretty short, between 7 and 11 seconds.

Bad voiceline: "No problem, Captain. I'll keep you covered while you take out that emplacement."

Better voiceline: "I've got you covered, Cap!"

In essence, the goal for these types of voicelines is to deliver as much pertinent information in as little time as possible. Try not to lengthen things through explanation or by adding too much detail.

Another good thing to do is to keep your voicelines as generic as possible. In this way, you can use them several times during the course of the game:

Player: "Jones! Stay here while I rescue the princess!"

Jones: "I've got you covered, Cap!"

Player: "I could really use a beer right now."

Jones: "I've got you covered, Cap!"

Of course, too many repetitions of "I've got you covered, Cap!" will make Jones sound like a parrot after a while, so you might want to mix it up with "gotcha!" and "Yessir!" once in a while.

Dialogue for Cutscenes

In many games, the designers use cutscenes to tell bits of story between gameplay. These cutscenes often depend on dialogue to show both character development and plot development while the player watches helplessly.

Conversations between characters in games can be difficult to write. As has been covered previously, the player is usually in no mood to put up with long conversations when his reflexes are ramped up from playing your game. In order to maintain the player's interest, your cutscenes have to be quick, full of information, and entertaining.

Writing entertaining dialogue is something screenwriters have been doing for many years. Reading books on how to write screenplays will help you fine-tune your skills in this area. However, here are some tips on things you should avoid:

Dialogue that doesn't further the conversation or deepen your knowledge of the characters should be left out as much as possible.

Princess: Jones! We have to find the Slug's secret weapon or the planet will be destroyed!

Princess: (Looking down at her dog, Biscuit) Oh, Biscuit! Naughty dog! You should never do that to mommy's shoes! Naughty Dog!

Princess: I think we may be able to find help if we can just contact my father's old friend, General Hammock!

Jones: Gotcha!

This would be better as:

Princess: Jones! If we can find my father's old friend, General Hammock, we can get help to locate the Slug's secret weapon and save the planet!

Jones: Gotcha!

Dialogue that explains the plot or repeats information the player already knows should be left out.

Princess: Jones! If we can find my father's old friend, General Hammock, we can get help to locate the Slug's secret weapon and save the planet!

Jones: Gotcha!

This would be better as:

Princess: Jones! General Hammock, my father's old friend, will help us! We need to find him!

Jones: Gotcha!

Unless there is some confusion as to who a character is talking to, try to keep from having one character name the other every time he talks to the other character.

Princess: Jones! General Hammock, my father's old friend, will help us! We need to find him!

Jones: Gotcha!

This would be better as:

Princess: General Hammock, my father's old friend, will help us! We need to find him!

Jones: Got ya covered!

Finally, try to avoid stilted, choppy speech whenever possible, unless that pattern is being used to identify a character trait.

Saturn-13: Biscuit! You're a naughty dog! Naughty! Naughty!

Biscuit: Bark! Bark!

Because the speakers here are characters that constantly use very short sentences, this could probably stay this way.

Writing Dialogue for Conversation Trees

No, I'm not talking about talking plants. Conversation trees are found in many role-playing and adventure games. Basically, they take a form such as the following:

Player activates an NPC in some way, causing him to talk.

NPC speaks an introductory sentence of some kind.

Player is given several choices of how he might respond:

> Choice 1
>
> Choice 2
>
> Choice 3

NPC responds to choice.

Player is either sent back to the first set of choices or given a new set.

And so on.

Conversation trees are a different breed of dialogue than the conversations that appear in other formats. For one thing, conversations like this can be a little longer. Usually, they appear in both written and text form so that the player can follow along at his own pace. Also, conversation trees are a form of gameplay in themselves: a clue search puzzle that the player gets to explore to learn new information about the game.

Here's an example:

Player: (Prods Saturn-13 to talk.)

Saturn-13: "Hello sir. How may I help you?"

Player Choice 1: "Do you know anything about the Slug's secret weapon?"

Player Choice 2: "What kind of robot are you?"

Player Choice 3: Exit conversation.

Saturn-13 Response 1: "How would I know? It is a secret."

Player Choice 1 to Response 1: "Oh, come on. You're a machine, it's a machine. Surely you know something."

Player Choice 2 to Response 1: Back to first level of conversation.

Player Choice 3 to Response 1: Exit conversation.

Saturn-13 Response 1a: (whispers) "I think you should take your racist ways and go back to the bridge."

Player Choice 1 to Response 1a: Back to first level of conversation.

Player Choice 2 to Response 1a: Exit conversation.

Saturn-13 Response 2: "I am a happy robot. Happy. Happy."

Player Choice 1 to Response 2: Back to first level of conversation.

Player Choice 2 to Response 2: Exit conversation.

As you can see, conversation trees can be confusing to build when they get complex. The more choices you give the player, the more responses you need to generate. Keeping all these lines under control—what the player says, how the NPC responds, where that response takes the player, what the player's choices are after that—is a lot like memorizing chess moves. Keeping them simple and shallow will help, as will writing them down on paper before you commit them to code.

It's also important that you include code that lets the player back up to previous levels of the tree. Being curious, the player usually wants to explore everything his conversation partner has to say. Allowing controls within the conversation tree to move back saves the player from having to exit the conversation and then go right back in again. Sometimes, this functionality can be hard-coded into a game. On the Xbox, for example, the B button on the controller is normally a "back" button, which allows you to go backward through trees like this, saving you the trouble of having to write conversation lines that have that functionality.

The same goes for exiting the conversation. You'll have to include that option unless the game engine has a hard-coded escape, such as the escape key on a PC.

Writing dialog for conversation trees still relies on your ability to keep things short and dense with information. While the lines can be a little longer than writing for cutscenes or in-game voicelines, the player still doesn't want to read more than a paragraph at one time.

Withering Branches

In conversation trees, many times you'll want a branch of conversation to go away. In many old adventure games, after the player has seen all the NPC has to say, the designer takes away the conversation tree and replaces it with a perfunctory one-liner that basically says "I've said all there is to say. Go somewhere else for more information."

There's a good side to this and a bad. The good is that you make that NPC like a check mark: The player can quickly determine whether he's spoken to this NPC and that he has all the information he's going to get out of him. The bad side is that the player can no longer access the voicelines that he read previously to remind him of information he may have forgotten.

In cases like this, it's always best to make the one-line answer a summation of what the player has gleaned from the NPC. For example:

Princess Gretchen: I told you I won't tell you anything more about the Slug Lord until you find my dog, Biscuit.

This line tells the player that the Princess will give him more information in the future and that one of the player's current missions is to find the Princess's missing dog.

Scripting Conversation Trees

Scripting conversation trees is pretty easy. Many games, like Bioware's *Neverwinter Nights*, do an excellent job at making conversations like this a breeze to build. The complexity that comes into these systems is from juggling variables.

Variables, as you know, are symbols that you can assign any value to. A variable named A could have a value such as 6, be assigned a formula such as $(c+d)/(x+y)$, or hold a string (a series of letters) such as "antidisestablishmentarianism."

When you use variables with conversation trees, their main use is as switches. These switches turn the appearance of different voicelines on and off. Here's an example using the variable A, which will start out with a value of true.

Player: (prods the Princess to speak)

Princess Gretchen: If *A* is true, then say "What can I do for you?"

This is followed by conversation that ends with her telling the player she won't tell him anything more unless he finds her dog. (change *A* to a value of false)

Princess Gretchen: If *A* is false, then say "I told you I won't tell you anything more about the Slug Lord until you find my dog, Biscuit."

Of course, this isn't the end of this tree. Now that the Princess has given a quest to the player, she now needs a set of voicelines that activates when the player gives her dog back to her. So a *B* variable set to true when the dog is found should be used.

As you can see, this can get pretty complicated very fast.

What You Have Learned

In this chapter, you should have learned the following concepts:

- That story for games is different from stories for other media because of the non-linear nature of games.
- How to create stories and place them for maximum effect when dealing with short attention spans.
- What types of stories go with what types of games.
- That stories in games are heavily concentrated around characters and what they do and say.
- The difference between character and characteristics.
- That showing, not telling, is the way to make the most out of your characters.
- What you can do to make a better villain.
- The what, why, and how of creating plots.
- How to create dialogue and keep it short and dense with information.
- How voicelines are used in games.
- Writing dialogue for in-game voicelines.
- Writing dialogue for cutscenes.
- Writing dialogue for conversation trees.
- The basics of scripting for conversation trees.

Review Questions

(Answers found in Appendix C)

1. What are the two main differences between stories for games and stories for movies or novels?
2. What clues does Maslow's hierarchy of needs give in telling stories in games?
3. All voicelines should have the same two qualities. What are they?
4. What are the six aspects of any plot?
5. A games relies mostly on what to tell the player its story?
6. Who is the most important character to develop in your game?
7. What are voicelines?
8. How long should in-game voicelines be?
9. What is a conversation tree?

On Your Own

1. If the toolset you're using allows for conversation trees, construct a conversation that "withers," or changes after the player has read through the conversation tree one time.
2. If the toolset you're using allows you to create cutscenes, create a cutscene of your character talking to a person who is giving him a mission. Try to make the person giving him the mission seem noble through his actions and words.
3. Write down a character trait, such as *noble* or *cruel*, and then write down all the things a person could do in a stressful situation that would show that trait to an audience.

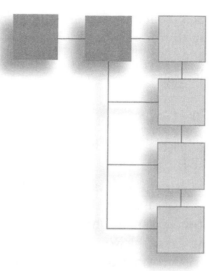

CHAPTER 9

POLISHING

Well, we've finally come to the end of the journey. Your terrain is laid down and textured. You have plants and animals and rocks and trees. Your architecture is standing bravely, ready to hold the adventures you've planned. All the enemies and puzzles are in place and are scripted to act just the way you want them to. You even have some story to go with it, maybe just an overarching theme, or maybe some dialogue or conversation trees.

But you're not done. Like building a sculpture, you've built your game's arms, legs, body, and head, but it still isn't perfect—it's still not fun.

In this chapter, you'll learn about

- polishing your level until it shines!
- testing your level
- some of the bugs you might expect to find in your level and some helpful suggestions on how to fix them
- balancing your gameplay
- why it's so important to have other people playtest your level

Repetition

Repetition is the key to polishing. Playing your game over and over is how you'll find the problems that plague it. Repeat battles over and over using every available weapon.

Scout out the edges of the map and see what you find there. Look everywhere for holes in your terrain or gaps in your architecture. By going over your level with a fine-tooth comb you'll be able to spot glaring problems and mistakes. In other words, test your level.

Testing

Quality assurance testing is a position that employs hundreds of people in the game industry. Both of the authors of this book started out as testers, as a matter of fact.

A professional tester does not have the best job out there, as some people may think. A tester has to sit in one place for many hours a week and play badly broken and frustrating games. Think about how you would feel if someone sat you down and made you play the worst game you could think of for 60 hours a week for 4 months straight. That's what a tester's job often is.

Understanding how professional test teams approach finding problems, or bugs, in games is a good way to sharpen your own skills at polishing your level. At the beginning of every game, everyone is a designer. At the end, everyone is a tester.

Test departments everywhere use two methods of testing: free testing and planned testing.

Free Testing

Free testing is pretty self-explanatory. The tester is allowed to roam as he will through the game, looking for mistakes. This method allows the tester to play the game as he normally would play it, but it also allows him to come up with strange and unique ways to play your game to see if it breaks it. For instance, the tester may try to do an entire level without killing something. He might race backward on the track, or he might try to talk to NPCs in reverse order. He'll try to get in places he shouldn't, jump from heights to see if they will kill his character, run into walls to see if they all have collision, and try to kill all the good guys. In doing this, the tester hopes to find all the bugs he can so they can be fixed, making for a better game.

The problem with this method is that it leaves gaps. In trying to find bugs in creative ways, the tester can miss things as he flits from one idea of how to break the game to the next. Also, if there are many testers using this method, there inevitably ends up being a lot of overlap as testers look for bugs in all the same places.

Planned Testing

Planned testing is a rigid process that usually relies on something called a test plan. A test plan is a list of tasks that a tester has to do in any given timeframe. A test plan can look like this:

1. Jump 100 times
2. Jump 100 times while firing shotgun
3. Jump 100 times while alternating firing shotgun and kicking
4. Jump 100 times while in cutscene

This type of testing is a bit more thorough than free testing. The person who creates the test plan, usually the lead tester, must break down everything he thinks a player can do in the game and create a task list to see if any of these things break the game. Testers then go out and do things like "Run into the building with the jeep 1000 times" and "Press the 'A' button as many times as you can while the game is loading."

The problem with test plans such as these is that they generally rely on one person to think of everything a player might do in the course of playing the game. Because of this, there might be gaps in those areas. That is why test departments try to balance the two testing types, planned and free, as the weaknesses of one are the strengths of the other.

Types of Bugs

Another thing that test departments do is classify their bugs. This allows them to prioritize them so that developers, artists, and designers know which bugs to fix first. Following is an example that some test departments use to classify their bugs.

- **"A" Bugs:** "A" bugs are bugs that keep the player from continuing with the game. They include bugs as obvious as crash bugs, which cause the game to halt in some drastic and violent way (a blue screen of death, for instance) to gameplay bugs that prevent the player from completing the game (there is no bridge between the side where the player starts and where the player is supposed to go, for example). "A" bugs are the highest priority to fix.
- **"B" Bugs:** "B" bugs are usually all the bugs in the game that don't prevent the player from finishing the game, but make the game harder or less fun to play. These can be bugs about objects with the wrong textures, landscapes or buildings that have gaps where you can see under or through something you shouldn't, a problem where the player runs out of ammunition before he can fight the final boss, or other similar bugs.

- **"C" Bugs:** "C" bugs usually end up being suggestion bugs, where the tester can place ideas for how he thinks the game could be better. Many of these actually get implemented, though not all do. It depends on the team and how good the idea is. Bugs that find themselves in this category are usually "Wouldn't it be cool if…" bugs, like "Wouldn't it be cool if the player could use a rocket launcher in both hands" or "It would be nice if the player could find a jeep here, as it takes too long for him to cross to the fortress by foot."

Designer as Tester

As the designer of your level or your game, you are the first person that will test your game. In professional environments, you will probably be assigning bugs to the programming and art teams well before a test team even sees your level. Because of this, it might be a good plan to learn the tricks that a tester uses to find all the holes in your level.

Start out by doing some free testing. Just play your level, going to all the areas and seeing if there are any problems. Play through it and see if you can beat the level and have it end correctly as you complete your mission. Make sure all your missions are correct.

After doing this, you might try some more structured testing. Make a list of everything you think could go wrong with your level and test those out, just as if you were going down a checklist. Don't try to do any of the heavy repetition stuff, like jumping up and down 1,100 times to see if the game will crash. If you are using a commercial toolset for an existing game, like the *Far Cry* Sandbox or *Half-Life* Source, then that kind of bug is in the code somewhere where you couldn't fix it. In any case, as a designer, you should be more worried about the people who play straight through your level than players who want to jump up and down thousands of times.

Once you find those bugs, write them down so you don't forget, and fix away!

Fixing Bugs

Because your level is a complex system made of different, interlocking subsystems (a combat system meshed with a movement system meshed with a 3D engine, etc.), bugs tend to be harder to fix than find.

Some bugs, like misplaced textures and objects whose placement obstructs the player from something, are pretty easy to fix. Other bugs, like bugs in your scripting or collision problems can be a lot harder to nail down.

Terrain Bugs

Terrain is usually the easiest thing to fix. The problems you'll usually find in terrain are gaps or holes that are showing the sky through the ground.

The first thing to do when you see these types of bugs is to reload and rebuild your geometry. These gaps are usually there because you've been editing it, and the engine hasn't caught up yet. Try rebuilding (as in having the engine rebuild it, not starting all over from scratch) and things usually turn out okay.

If you still have problems, you might have too many sharp angles in your terrain. Smooth it out some to see if the engine can cope with shallower angles.

Finally, if even that doesn't work, you might consider building a huge plane, colored black or, if you only have one terrain texture, like grass, color it to match that. Then, slip the plane under your terrain. If there any gaps, at least they won't show blue sky through them.

Architecture Bugs

Architecture bugs come in three forms: gaps, normals, and collision problems.

- Gaps are when there is a slight space between two pieces of architecture, like a corner of a room, or between a doorjamb and a wall.

- When I talk about "normal" problems, I am referring to the fact that a piece of 3D geometry usually has a surface that you can see, and a surface that you can't. Normals are usually represented by a series of arrows coming away from the object. The arrows point away from the side of the object you can see. If you look at the other side, the object turns invisible. If you are in a piece of architecture and you are seeing through a wall that should be there, then you have a normal facing the wrong way.

- Collision in games is the force that stops the player from walking through an object. Much like you would collide and stop when you walk into a wall in real life, a character in a game would hit an object's collision and stop. Collision is constantly calculated in a game, and a lot of objects with collision can add up to really drag down your performance. Because of this, collision in games can be a different shape than the object it is associated with. This different shape may give an object places to collide that the player can't see. For instance, in some games, cars just use a big rectangle for collision. This means that, even though it looks like you could slide something underneath a car, the collision area may be low enough to the ground that the object you tried to slide may just bounce off thin air.

Fixing Gaps

Gaps are pretty easy to understand how to fix, but can be very hard to do. The answer is usually to try and finesse two objects closer together so the gap disappears. Depending on the gap, you can sometimes intersect the two offending objects and no one will be the wiser. However, if you try to meld two objects, such as inserting two duplicate wall plates into each other to make a wall only one-and-a-half times the size of one of the plates, you'll end up with a sorting bug. Sorting is when the engine can't tell which object is in front of which and will keep switching them as the player looks on, causing a kind of twitchy flashing look.

A better way to fix the bug is see if the toolset has ways of making your control over objects slower. When you began working with your level, it was good to be able to drag a piece of architecture across the screen as fast as you could move your mouse, but now, when you need finesse, a slower speed is more useful.

A good tip for this type of work is to see if you can group your individual objects. Grouping sticks all the objects in your group together, making the whole thing seem like one piece. This is useful when moving walls because you'll inevitably end up closing up one gap while opening one up on the other side. Grouping things together makes fixing this type of thing easier.

If you find that you have two pieces of architecture that just do not want to fit together without creating more bugs, the black plane trick works just as well with architecture. Make a black plane and stick it behind the crack. Players will just assume that the lighting isn't good enough to see in there and go back to playing your game.

Fixing Normals

As stated above, a normal bug is one where the player is seeing through something he shouldn't be. Most objects are one-sided: you can only see them from one side. Sometimes, players will be able to get in to places where they can see through something they shouldn't.

The easiest way to fix something like this is to cover it up. Slap something in front of that hole so it's blocking any gaps.

A harder way to do this is to find a replacement object with two sides (with normals pointing out both directions, for example). This is probably the preferred way to handle this, but isn't always something you can do. It may require an artist to create that two-sided object for you, which may not be possible if you're just building a mod in your free time.

A final solution is to set up your level so the player can't even get to the spot where he can see, or actually can't see, the offending object. This is probably the least preferred way of taking care of this kind of problem.

Fixing Collision

Collision problems are evil. Sometimes, there's no explanation for it... a shard of something interacts with something else and suddenly your character can't walk through an open doorway, or the character walks through stairs instead of climbing on top of them.

If you're using a commercial toolset and objects from the original game, you might not have any recourse but to make your level in a different way to avoid the problem. However, there are some things you can try before you go that far.

Try deleting the offending object and replacing it again. This works in a lot of cases. If that doesn't work, try removing it altogether and see if the collision problem remains. If it does, then painstakingly search for the offending item. Save your level, delete an item, test it. If the problem persists, reload your level, delete another item, rinse, and repeat.

Sometimes a good way to fix this is to take away the offending object's collision. Some toolsets allow you to take away collision in its properties. If the object didn't need collision anyway, like a doorjamb (a character's shoulder brushing *through* a doorjamb is an oft-occurring thing in 3D games), then leave it be. If it does need collision (like a wall), then you can build new collision for it, or even take an object of similar size and shape, place it in the exact same spot as the bad object, and turn it invisible. Many times in games the collision of an object stays even when the player can't see it.

Collision on moving objects is probably the most problematic. If you have a door that has problems with collision, a sneaky trick is to place an invisible, static object in the door. When the player tries to interact with the door, destroy or teleport the invisible object so it's no longer in the way. This isn't the best method of doing things, since it takes a lot of finesse and may cause other problems, such as a dip in performance, but it is an answer for when you're desperate.

Placement and AI bugs

Placement bugs are easy to fix: Place whatever the problem is somewhere else. However, when it's the function of those objects, how they work, or their AI, then the problem becomes more complicated.

In most cases, problems with objects the player can interact with, like enemies or buttons, lies in their scripting, or what you're programming their functionality to be.

Sometimes, however, an object's AI can give you problems. Perhaps you have a guard walking through places he shouldn't, falling down wells, or even walking through walls. If this is the case, check the object's controls. See if you can't restrain his pathing so that he won't walk anywhere or not walk beyond a certain distance.

If the guard is pathing between waypoints—basically, little points that you place for the unit to know when he's gotten to a destination and now has to walk towards the next one on the list—then fiddle with the placement of the waypoints to see if he can't path better.

If the toolset doesn't have easy controls like this, then you'll probably have to create a script to control the guard in a tighter grip.

Locks that don't work and buttons that won't press can also be a problem. Make sure the player can "see" the object as something he can interact with. If he can't, then you might have placed the lock as a regular, no-special-abilities static object. If he can, but the lock doesn't push or the lock doesn't open, check the object's properties and see that they are set correctly. If that seems okay, check to see if there's a script involved and find out if there are any problems. Maybe the lock only becomes active once a button is pushed somewhere, and that object's functionality is broken.

Finally, for any placed item problem, check your portals and occluders to see if the object is on the cusp of two areas, or is trying to move between them. The connection point between two areas can nullify the interactivity of an object when it's not sure whether it's supposed to be in one or the other.

Scripting Bugs

99% of all scripting bugs have to do with the following three things:

1. Misspelled words
2. Extra or missing punctuation
3. Bad use of lower case or capital letters in case-sensitive languages like LUA

That's right, every time a script doesn't work the way you tell it to, those are the first three things to look for.

Usually, if a toolset gives you a line number where it thinks something is wrong, and you check that line and it looks fine, then check the line immediately previous to it. It's likely that there's a punctuation error that's knocked everything off balance afterwards.

Another common problem is misspelling your variables, either by just plain getting them wrong, or by putting a capital letter where a lower case letter is supposed to be. Whenever possible while scripting, cut and paste your variables into place rather than typing them out. That can really help. This also goes for function names. *Especially* for function names.

Sometimes a script won't work because it is depending on another script to switch a variable from one value to another. Check all the scripts your script is dependent on to make sure they are firing.

Scripting bugs are sometimes so glaringly obvious that you can't see them. If you're having problems with a script, and just can't figure it out, have a friend look at it. I can't tell you how many times I've run to a programmer with some scripting problem, and, upon seeing my code, he says, "You left out some quotation marks right there." Embarrassing! But I couldn't have done it any other way.

Balancing

While you are working through your game, you might notice that some things are too easy, and some things are too hard. Trying to make everything just right is called "balancing."

Balancing your game can be difficult because of the many things that are interconnected. Altering the player's ability to affect the game in order to prepare him for one encounter, such as giving him better weapons or more health, can make all other encounters seem too easy. Making an individual encounter easier or harder, such as reducing hit points or armor of a foe, can lead to the expectation that all similar encounters should be the same difficulty, which can lead to disappointed players.

Here's a good plan for balancing your game:

1. Start with trying to get a feel for the overall difficulty of the level. Is it too easy? Too hard? Adjust the player's power to try to make the world balance out. Give the player more health, or give out more ammunition or health packs.

2. When that feels good, try to identify the "bumps and dips" of your level: individual encounters that seem too easy or too hard. Try to reduce or increase the number of enemies the player faces. Try to resist making global changes to enemies, unless you are responsible for the difficulty level of those enemies for every level of your game.

3. If bumps and dips remain, where the balance is such that by removing something or adding something the balance is completely knocked off, go for too difficult and then put a small helper near the area, like a health pack, to even things out.

Once you've got things just about right, it's time to get another person to test it.

Have Another Person Test Your Level

By the time you are finished putting in your terrain and architecture, placed all your enemies and scripted them just right, you have completely lost all ability to look at your level objectively.

It's not your fault. I'm sure, in ordinary circumstances, you are as objective as Mr. Spock from *Star Trek*. However, when it comes to your level, you are so knowledgeable about its inner workings, and so enmeshed in the gameplay you've been trying to create, that it's mentally impossible for you to distance yourself from it.

This is why you need other people, perhaps many other people, to play your level and give you feedback.

When I was a new level designer, I worked on a level until I felt it was pretty good. One day, I went down to the testing area and stood behind a tester as he played through my level. He did it all wrong! He was *supposed* to fly one way, but he flew in a different direction. All the turrets I put down to "direct his path" he considered a challenge and made sure to hunt quite a few down. He didn't find the powerup I'd thought was in an obvious place. I was quite upset.

And then I realized that a lot of people were probably going to play my level exactly as this tester did. Having another person play my level really opened my eyes.

So, when you are done with your level, start asking other people to play through it. Ask nicely, and ask for feedback. If you can, watch them play your level. Half of the difficulties they encounter won't be visible to them. They'll just think that the missile that kills them every time is just another part of the game.

More importantly, when watching them play your level, don't say a word.

You'll want to. You'll be dying, trying not to tell them to turn a certain way, or use a certain weapon, or nudge them to go to one encounter before they go to a second. Oh, you'll *burn*!

But you can handle it. It'll open your eyes.

Example   169

If your level is a multiplayer map, put it where people can get at it and, if possible, play in viewer mode. Just keep flitting around your map and see if there's a spot that, if a player camps that spot, he owns your game. See if one side is getting better weapons quicker. See if there are areas where people get stuck, or lost. Take notes. Afterwards, release version 1.1 with all the problems fixed.

If your game is an RTS, make sure that everyone's ramp-up time is about equal. Make sure your terrain doesn't have a frustrating amount of blind alleys or impassable terrain. Watch to see if one side seems to become powerful earlier due to some aspect of how you placed your resources.

And, of course, make sure everyone is having fun.

Some Problems Are Actually Features

It's tempting to continue to refine a level until it becomes featureless. Like a sculpture worked on and worked on until the nose becomes too small to be a nose anymore, your level needs to be at least somewhat frustrating for players. Walks in the park are fun once, but a challenge takes time to defeat, and then, if it's really good, it's fun just to beat it again and again just to show off your mastery.

It's okay to make your game a little too tough.

Example

Okay, it's time to start making our level ready for prime time. I went through the level we made in Chapter 8, and found some serious bad mojo.

The first thing I found was that, on my decrepit 1.8 gigahertz machine, the game ran slow as molasses in the editor when I looked in the forest (see Figure 9.1).

The best thing to do was to start playing around with different settings until I found one that worked.

I started by removing the tree's abilities to cast shadow maps. Didn't make a dent. I went further and got rid of most of the tree's shading abilities. It was still slow, and the forest didn't look as good anymore.

I then decided that maybe I could lose some of the grass, so I got rid of about half of it. I also ended up changing the sky to something darker so the player wouldn't notice the lack of cool dynamic shading.

It was still pretty slow, but, in the end, it was a bit better (see Figure 9.2).

Figure 9.1 Actual framerate of level.

Figure 9.2 Now with 50% less grass for those who want low-carb *Far Cry* action.

Example   171

The next thing I found was a missing wall piece. When making the elevator, that particular wall piece's collision was preventing the elevator from getting to the top, and we forgot to put something there to replace it (see Figure 9.3). Totally amateur hour on that one. I left the lack of the wall in the Chapter 8 example for you to look at and giggle at our ineptitude.

Figure 9.3 An example of one-sided objects. The walls around the elevator house are invisible from the inside. The lines visible in the air are the edges of the walls.

To fix it, I just found the same object we used before and replaced it: a wall with a door hole in it that matched the surrounding walls. Surprisingly, the new wall didn't have the same collision problem as the other wall (see Figure 9.4).

Another bug that's been with us for a while is that the occluder for the interior section of the level didn't have a portal in the elevator shaft. This was giving the player this lovely view of the inside of the hill when he was raised about halfway up (see Figure 9.5).

Figure 9.4 Fixed elevator house. Also, a good look at the new sky.

Figure 9.5 Interior of a mountain. You'd think there'd be more rock.

Example   173

By placing a portal in the elevator shaft, the interior section and the exterior section blended, and the problem was solved (see Figure 9.6).

Figure 9.6 The whole elevator shaft. Beautiful!

Of course, there is still a lot left to do in this level to make it playable. We'd like to work on the pathing of the mutants in the forest. The end combat was a little less... talky... than I wanted it, and I'm not sure Prospero is well represented as a 7-foot mutant with a gun melded to his hand. There's still the framerate problem, and the pigs just aren't mean enough. I guess all that will have to wait for "Intermediate Game Level Design."

What You Have Learned

In this chapter, you learned the following concepts:

- Fixing bugs is an important part of polishing your level
- Free testing and planned testing

- The three levels of bugs: A, B, and C
- Types of terrain bugs and some suggestions on how to fix them
- Types of architecture bugs, like gaps, normals, and collision problems, and how to approach fixing them
- Placement and AI bugs, and some suggestions on how to fix them
- Scripting bugs and the three most common mistakes, bad spelling, bad punctuation, and incorrect case
- How to balance your level
- Why it's important to have other players test your level

Review Questions

(Answers can be found in Appendix C)

1. What is the key to having a solid game?
2. What is the difference between free testing and planned testing?
3. What is an "A" bug?
4. If you see a gap in your terrain, what should you do to try and fix it?
5. If you have a normal problem, how should you go about fixing it?
6. Name the three most common problems that cause scripts not to work.
7. Why is it important to have another person test your level?

On Your Own

1. If you are using the *Far Cry* Sandbox, go to our Chapter 8 example and see if you can fix the same bugs we did for this chapter.
2. Go to your level and find 10 problems with it and write them down.
3. Have another person play your level. Keep quiet as they play through it. Write down all the problems they encounter while playing your game.
4. Look at your list of 10 problems and compare it to the list you generated while watching the other person play. How many of those things match? Take both lists, add them together, and prioritize them. Which list has more entries in the top 10? Your list or the other one?

CHAPTER 10

SPECIFIC GENRES

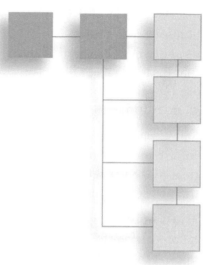

So far, we've been concentrating mostly on very general information about level design. We wanted to do that because we didn't want to make a "how-to" book for a specific editor or genre. This chapter is an attempt at rectifying that a little by going over specific genres of games, and laying out some design tips for them. We'll also try to include the names of games you can look for that have editors available for them, so you can try your hand at them if you feel like experimenting.

Action Games

Action games are games that tend to be very character based, usually taking place in real-time. Types of action games include first-person shooters, third-person action adventures, locked position (or rail) shooters, fighting games, and platformers.

First-Person Shooters

Almost all first-person shooters come with an editor, and the mod community for these games is huge! There are tons of people out there who spend their time creating levels, both good and bad for this genre. Because of this, there are many places you can place your game so that people can download and play it.

Designing for FPSs is really split between single-player and multiplayer design.

Single-Player Design for FPSs

Single-player design is what we've been focusing on throughout this book. The designer needs to focus a lot on the challenges that the player will face and make sure that his level layout is friendly enough so the player won't get lost. Single-player games are very much focused on the main character and trying to immerse the player in the game world.

Single-player FPSs are story-oriented, but are hard to put story into because they are so fast paced. When making games like this, try to lay most of your story on the setting: Make the setting of your game show the story elements rather than trying to tell the player everything.

The flow of a single-player level can be very linear, with a start and a finish to it. This helps you reinforce the story, as there will be a beginning, middle, and an end. This doesn't mean you can't have some more interesting side areas to explore, special items to find, and more, but keep it reasonable, and avoid making those side areas mandatory to completion, as not all players will find them.

Multiplayer Design for FPSs

Multiplayer design is very different from single-player design. For one thing, you can throw story right out the door. Multiplayer maps are all about people competing against other people, so you don't have to worry about entertaining the player with your delightful storytelling abilities.

When designing multiplayer maps, for fast-paced shooters like *Unreal* and *Quake*, the flow of the map should be pretty circular, as these games tend to have a lot of running around in them. There shouldn't be any dead ends (unless that dead end has a benefit to it, like being a good ambush point or sniper spot), and you should continually watch for places in the level that are hard to move around.

FPS games that rely on bases, such as the *Battlefield* games or *Tribes*, tend to have bigger maps with defensible spots in them. These defensible spots should favor the base they are nearest to.

Fairness is the key issue in multiplayer design. Your map can't have any areas that allow one person or side to dominate the game (unless the challenge of the level is to overcome a superior force). Weapons should be freely available to any faction or player if they know where to look.

Cooperative Design for FPSs

Some FPS games allow cooperative play, such as the game *Halo*. Designing levels for this type of play is very similar to designing for single-player levels, except everything needs to be adjusted in terms of difficulty to give an acceptable challenge to larger numbers of players.

If your level will be cooperative play only, try to create gameplay that requires teamwork to do, like having to activate two machines at the same time, or having suppression fire actually mean something in your game.

First-Person Shooters with Editors

Aliens Vs Predator 2	Sierra Studios	Monolith Productions
Battlefield 1942	EA Games	Digital Illusions
Battlefield Vietnam	EA Games	Digital Illusions
Chaser	Encore Software, Jowood Productions	Cauldron Limited
Deus Ex	EIDOS Interactive	ION Storm
Duke Nukem 3D		
Duke Nukem Manhattan Project	Arush	Sunstorm Interactive
FarCry	Ubisoft	Crytek Studios
Half-Life	Valve	Sierra Studios
Max Payne (PC)	Gathering of Developers	3D Realms and Remedy Entertainment
Medal of Honor	EA Games	Dreamworks Interactive
No One Lives Forever Series	Monolith Productions	Sierra Studios, Fox Interactive, Vivendi Universal Games
Painkiller	Dreamcatcher	People Can Fly
Quake	id	Activision
Savage	S2	S2
Serious Sam (PC)	Croteam	Gathering of Developers
Thief series	ION Storm	EIDOS Interactive
Timesplitters 1	EIDOS Interactive	Free Radical Design
Timesplitters 2	EIDOS Interactive	Free Radical Design
Starsiege TRIBES	Dynamix	Sierra Studios
Tribes 2	Dynamix	Sierra Studios
Tribes: Vengeance	Irrational Games	Vivendi Universal Games
TRON 2.0	Monolith Productions	Buena Vista Interactive
Unreal Series	Epic	Atari

Third-Person Games

The over-the-shoulder camera in this game genre is something that bears a lot of consideration in your design. The player loses his ability to aim really well, as in FPSs, and gains the ability to see his own character and what's directly behind him.

The player being able to see his avatar is a two-sided sword. The good side is that it helps the player care more for his avatar, as a reader would care about a character from a book. It allows the designer to give the avatar a personality of his own, which the player will accept. In first person, the player thinks of his avatar as "me." In third person, the player finds it easier to distance himself from the avatar and begin thinking in terms of "him." Once this happens, the avatar can say things without the player being turned off by the designer putting words in his mouth.

The other edge of this sword is that the avatar has to be the best-looking thing in the game. The player is always looking at it; so it needs to have the most polygons and the best animations; whereas in a first-person game, all you need is a good-looking hand and gun. Having this very expensive avatar model means that the rest of the game loses much ability in terms of its art and animations.

The camera is also a bit of a loose cannon in third-person games, as it can get into positions where the player can't see at all.

Third-person cameras generally are made with collision, just like the player. If they weren't, the players would frequently be looking through walls and ceilings and through enemies as the camera moved through them. Sometimes this collision is done well, and you don't notice it; other times, the camera ends up in a corner as the player is trying to get around something, and suddenly, all you see is the avatar's back.

One other area where camera can be a major challenge in games like this is with "bosses." As a general rule, most games tend to change camera behavior when fighting bosses to focus on a point halfway between the main character and the boss. This can cause a lot of problems and become a major challenge to presenting the visual data you want or need. This is an issue to be very aware of when doing these types of encounters, as the presentation of your bosses can easily make or break a game.

When you build environments for third-person games, be sure to pay extra attention to how the camera acts so you can adjust your terrain or architecture to compensate.

Third-person games are usually hybrid games that combine adventure elements, platformer puzzles, and action. This means your job as a designer will be extra challenging because you'll want to design physical puzzles, combat challenges, and story elements into your game. This can be a lot of work.

Third-Person Games with Editors

Star Trek: Deep Space Nine The Fallen (PC)	The Collective Simon & Schuster Interactive	
Freedom Force	Irrantional Games	EA Games
RUNE	Human Head Studios	Gathering of Developers
Tenchu 2	Acquire	Activision

Locked-Position Shooters

Also called a rail shooter, this type of game is basically a shooting gallery on wheels. Level design for this type of game is mostly target placement and setting up the rail that carries the player along.

Because the player has a simple interface, basically swiveling and firing, you are able to throw a lot more action at him. Further, because you always know where he is, the linear nature makes it easy to gauge the difficulty ramp of an individual level better than in games where the player gets to wander around.

Usually, when you can decide on a difficulty ramp like this, you'll want a two-bump curve: The level increases in difficulty as the player goes along and then peaks about halfway through. The player gets a rest, and then the difficulty ramps up again until the climax of the level. This gives the level a nice sense of pacing. See Figure 10.1 for an example.

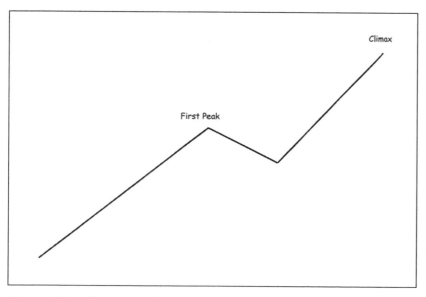

Figure 10.1 Illustration of a two-bump difficulty curve.

The action of a level has a minor peak somewhere around the halfway point, and then backs off for a bit before ramping up to the final climax.

Rail shooters also have a pretty established flow as a genre. Usually, the player fights a bunch of low-level minions, which become more numerous and more difficult as the level moves on, until the player is literally swarmed. Once he defeats this, the level either caps off with a boss monster fight, or the player goes to a new level where he only fights a boss monster.

One of the things to really look at in this type of game is save points. Usually, rail shooters don't have a save anywhere feature, which means the designer has to decide where the player's progress is saved. Having the game save right before a big boss fight is probably the nicest thing you can do for the player in a game of this type.

Fighting Games

Fighting games like *Mortal Kombat*, *Tekken*, and *Virtua Fighter* belong to this category. Fighting games feature two or more combatants involved in hand-to-hand fighting.

Design for these games is usually concerned more with balancing each fighter against the others so she will feel unique, but be pretty equal in power. Because of the sheer numbers of combinations and moves a character in one of these games has, it becomes an incredible task to figure out how to do this.

Fighting games tend to be pretty resistant to story. Players are more concerned with learning A+A+B+Y+R+R+L+⑧+■ to pay attention to much more. Usually, story gets shoved in post-fight cutscenes and character bios.

Talking about combinations, the players of these types of games usually are either very, very good, with godlike reflexes and a mimetic memory that allows them to shoot off huge combos without even thinking or Neanderthals like me that mash on one button a lot and hope to win.

Because of this wide variation in skill levels, you'll need to design the game so that both these types of players find the game fun. This can be quite a challenge, usually involving the creation of a difficulty system and several levels of reactive AI.

Fighting Games with Level Editors

One Must Fall: Battlegrounds   Diversions Entertainment

Platformers

Platform games generally rely on jumping puzzles, some combat, and player-determined pacing as their core gameplay.

Platformers are usually fairly linear, the player having to defeat a series of puzzles and challenges in a certain order to progress through the game. While not as linear as the rail shooter, it still holds enough structure to hold a classically built sequential story. Also like the rail shooter, a two-peak difficulty ramp serves nicely to pace the action of a level.

Because platformers rely so much on jumping and movement puzzles, a designer needs to have a solid understanding of the capabilities of the main character. He needs to know exactly how far the character can jump, how fast he can run, and how much space the character takes up. Every single maneuver the player can make should be closely measured so that puzzles can be made that are challenging but not impossible.

Due to this, platform games have a heavily emphasized paper development phase, where the designer uses graph paper to chart out exactly the amount of space a level will take up, as well as how far apart jumping platforms will be, how high ceilings will be, and so on.

Save points in platformers usually occur at the beginning/end of a level, but you might see one somewhere in between. Always err on the side of having too many save points than too few.

2D Action Games

In the late '80s and throughout the '90s, side-scrolling platformers and shooters became extremely popular. Platformers like Nintendo's *Mario* games, Sega's *Sonic* games, along with shooters like the *1941* series and many others drove the sales of many game consoles.

Today, games like this can still be found on handhelds like the Gameboy Advance and DS, as well as many cell phones. There are even some free tools out there that allow you to create these types of games.

Side-scrolling games generally are extremely action-oriented and linear. Because of the fast-paced nature of the games, and the limited amount of computer processor power and memory, these games were short on story, but long on action.

Like 3D platformers, games like this use a lot of paper design to show how the player is going to progress through each area.

Difficulty ramping, is, again, easily accomplished because of the linearity of the game. Like rail shooters, 2D games like this love having big bosses at the ends of levels to provide the climactic challenge.

Save points in these types of games were usually only located at the beginnings of new levels, though some had other systems that were a bit more forgiving.

2d Scrolling Toolsets

Scrolling Game Development Kit   http://gamedev.sourceforge.net/index.shtml   Benjamin Marty

Strategy Games

Strategy games are one of the few genres of games that are still primarily focused on the PC, rather than having moved over to the more lucrative console systems.

Mod making for strategy games is very popular, with most RTS games coming out with an accompanying editor.

Creating mods for strategy games requires an intimate knowledge of the mechanics of that game. Without a firm grasp of the intricacies of the balancing between the different units available, and the types of terrain they master or find themselves weak in, your attempts at creating levels may lead to huge imbalances that tip the map unexpectedly towards one type of unit or strategy.

Knowing the gameplay tactics of those who have mastered these games is also handy when designing, as you'll have a good idea of what types of terrain and setting help either facilitate or derail those tactics.

Story in strategy games usually takes place between battles, though at times there might be a cutscene that takes place right after a climactic spot in a level.

All strategy games rely heavily on very smart AI. Designing mods for strategy games is pretty easy in this regard, as you can usually just set down the beginnings of a force wherever you want them to start, and they'll take care of the rest. Even scripting paths for units so you can do "patrols" and the like tends to be fairly simple to achieve in most cases.

Strategy games, mostly turn-based and real time, use tiles to create their terrain, which also adds to the ease of creating mods for them.

Although most games require an element of strategy, in this section we'll just cover turn-based, real-time, and 4X strategy games.

Real-Time Strategy Games

Modern real-time strategy games are all about insane levels of micromanagement. The player controls a large number of individual units, which he deploys on a field of battle against one or more opponents. When you boil it down, RTS games have three areas that require intense concentration from a designer.

- **Balancing.** RTS games must feel fair. Feeling fair is different than being fair, because, in order for someone to feel a game is fair, it means that they actually feel it is balanced in their favor. This is a kind of a paradox, but it's true. The player at all times should feel that he is empowered and ahead of the game in some respect.

  This is a very hard feat to accomplish. It means that not only must you design units that are balanced against the other units in the game, but you must also make them feel cool. Players must feel that their choice of units is tactically strong, and that they can win with those units given certain circumstances.

  A good way to achieve this feeling is to implement a rock-paper-scissors strategy to your balancing. In the game rock-paper-scissors, a circular pattern is established in terms of victory and defeat with scissors beating paper, paper beating rock, and rock beating scissors. In an RTS game, perhaps cavalry beats infantry, which beat pike men, which beat cavalry. However, this gets a lot more complex when you start considering all the individual units across the breadth of the game.

- **AI.** Artificial intelligence becomes easier to program when the designer has a good idea of his balancing system. If your programmers know exactly how each unit is supposed to act in combat, it frees up some of their time to implement important, game-making-or-breaking features like pathing. Balancing units isn't the only thing a designer has to think of when it comes to AI, however. You also have to think of how units act in all sorts of situations. Do they ever retreat? What is their opening strategy or build order? When do they know it's a good time to expand to a second or third or fourth base? What units does each side favor? Does this change with difficulty level? Answering these questions in a way that makes the game fun for the player is a tough, brain-straining job that takes a lot of iteration to get right. This is why a lot of the best RTS games spend months on just testing and balancing after the game has pretty much been finished.

- **Interface.** The interface of an RTS is also a make-or-break feature. The gameplay of these games usually is comprised of selecting units or buildings and giving them commands. These units are usually not all in the player's immediate view and he has to chase them down before he can give them commands. Luckily, most RTS games are heading toward a somewhat standard interface, so many of these things have already been thought of and applied to the games that are out there right now. Using those standards will help you make your game accessible to veterans of the genre.

For designers who just want to do multiplayer maps for existing RTS games, you really don't have to worry about AI, balancing, and interface at all, as these things have been done already in the making of the core game for which you are designing the map. The elements you have to look into are enemy camp placement, resource placement, and terrain strategy.

- **Enemy camp placement.** This is both easy and hard. Easy in that you can just place each camp as far away from the next one as you want. Hard in that you'll have to design your terrain to accommodate that, plus you'll have to place resources as close to each base as to every other base. Assuring everybody starts on an equal foot is the essence of placing starting positions.

- **Resource placement.** Beginning resources do not necessarily have to be in a convenient place for each player to get initially, but too much frustration will send players seeking maps that allow them a quicker start-up.

- **Terrain strategy.** Terrain in RTS games needs to be strategically interesting. By this I mean that the terrain should have areas that allow advantages and disadvantages for defenders and attackers. Having bottlenecks, hills, valleys, unassailable cliffs, open plains, and islands are some of the terrain features you can place to make your map more interesting.

Fog of War

Most RTS games do not show the entire game map. As the player explores, he exposes the terrain features hidden in this "fog of war." Anything you place outside the player's immediate viewing range is a thing that he must explore to find. On the other hand, any player who has played on that map will have the advantage of knowing where things are located. If you place resources or other important items in places that are hidden at the start of a game, it gives the experienced player an incredible advantage over new players (or players with terrible memories).

Usually, on balanced maps, all players start in easily defendable areas. This creates gameplay where each side has a fairly strong position creating units to conquer weaker positions further inside the map. Games that take place on maps like these can create exciting combat situations as land and resources get traded back and forth among opponents.

Unbalanced maps can also be exciting if the players know what they are getting in to and have the option to choose who has the advantage and who doesn't. A map where one side is trying to overcome a tactically superior position, like a hilltop fortress, can be very fun. The side assaulting the base gets free reign of the land, and thus any resources that might be there, while the hilltop's defenders get a tactically superior position and some pre-built fortifications. A good thing to add in unbalanced maps is a time limit—to add some urgency to the attacker's need to overcome his foe.

Real-Time Strategy Games with Editors

Advance Wars 2 (Gameboy)	Nintendo	Nintendo
Age of Empires series	Microsoft	Ensemble Microsoft
Command & Conquer: Generals	EA Games	Electronic Arts Pacific
Starcraft	Blizzard Entertainment, Vivendi Universal Games	
Total War Series	Creative Assembly Activision, Inc., EA Games	
Warcraft Series	Blizzard Entertainment, Vivendi Universal	

Turn-Based Strategy Games

Turn-based strategy games are slow-paced strategy games that allow players to take their time and decide what they want to do before acting. The game pauses while the player decides what he wants his troops to accomplish. After the first player uses up all his time, the next player gets to choose his unit's actions. This goes on until all sides have taken their turns. The computer then moves everything at once, determines the outcomes of any combat that takes place, and then shows that information to the player. The player then gets to take his turn again.

Because of this slow, halting pace, turn-based games where turns are longer than a couple minutes tend not to be very popular as multiplayer games. Thus, the single-player game is usually where the concentration for these types of games lies.

Because the player gets more time to consider his options, turn-based games usually have a greater range of options and scope than RTS games. While RTS games tend to concentrate on one plot of land, turn-based games can take place over entire continents or worlds. Whereas RTS units have one or two abilities or uses, units in turn-based games can have several. The same goes for depth of strategic decisions. Players of turn-based games are able to concentrate on tactics far more than RTS players, meaning that the AI in these games needs to think more along those lines as well.

For designers who are just making maps for turn-based games, the main emphasis is to create interesting tactical challenges for the player. Although complex, multifaceted maps are possible, most amateur maps delve into the "what if" category where single scenarios are built to experiment with different configurations of troops along with terrain that has been painstakingly reproduced from real life or built to demonstrate some interesting advantage or disadvantage.

Turn-Based Strategy Games with Editors

Civilization 2	MicroProse Software, Inc.	
Civilization 3	Infogrames	
Alpha Centauri	EA Games	Firaxis Games
Heroes of Might and Magic III and IV	New World Games	3DO

Role-Playing Games

Role-playing games concentrate on character growth and story to enhance their gameplay. Generally, the player is allowed a good amount of customization in the creation and development of the character, with the ability to choose the character's appearance and beginning abilities. These abilities classically come in the form of statistics, which determine how proficient the character is at interacting with the world.

RPGs are some of the largest games available, having hundreds of hours of gameplay within them. Because of this, they also tend to have thousands and thousands of individual objects and sounds created for them as the designers try to populate entire continents and worlds. Just keeping track of these multitudes is a full-time job—along with giving each item whatever functionality it might have, from just being a decorative object meant to add to the ambiance, to weapons, to objects that enhance the character's statistics. Truly, in these types of games, the database becomes the designer's best friend.

The story in RPGs is the core to their design. The overarching plot becomes a reef where a coral of subquests and encounters grows. Mechanics form the glue, which sticks everything together, but mechanics are usually created out of necessity to serve the central theme. Want the player to fight dragons? Create the mechanics. Want them to be able to shoot laser guns AND use swords? Create those mechanics too. This is unlike many other games, like sports games or racing games, where the story serves the mechanics (we've made this great fighting game, let's slap a story on it!).

RPGs usually come in two forms, the Japanese-style RPG and the Western RPG. By Western, I mean European/North American style, not cowboy-style.

- **Japanese-style RPGs** are very linear and cling to the central story very tightly. Side-quests are few and far between. This style RPG, perhaps best represented by Square/Enix's *Final Fantasy* series, uses many detailed cutscenes interspersed with very controlled combat environments to tell their story as the player is led through a series of environments.

- **Western RPGs** were originally created to mimic the gameplay of pen and paper role-playing games, like *Dungeons and Dragons*. Because of this, these games are decidedly non-linear, only controlling the player's direction through the use of unlocking quests and using the character growth (or lack thereof) as a limiting factor to keep the player from accessing parts of the game the designers don't want to reveal too soon. For example, when entering a new region of forest, the player is assaulted by creatures much too powerful for him to fight. He manages to run away, but makes a note to himself to check the place out once his character is more powerful. By structuring areas to be accessible to a certain power level, the designers force a rudimentary linearity on the player. This method is not infallible. Players have ways of getting around your carefully laid plans and discovering things they aren't supposed to, which means you need to stick another system in place that further structures your game. In the case of RPGs, that system would be the *quest* system.

Quests are found in practically all RPGs in some form or another. A quest is basically a task that the player must perform in order to get some sort of reward. In RPGs, quests are laid out in such a way that they can reveal bits of story in the appropriate order. For instance, a fairly standard set of tasks and rewards might be:

1. Player is sent to kill a series of vermin-class creatures. Upon fulfilling this quest, he is given a better weapon and scroll to take to the next town.

2. Player takes scroll to next town. Upon delivery, the player sees a cutscene that shows the beginning of the overarching plot. A secret society of do-gooders has noticed The Coming of Darkness. Player is given a nice protective item and sent to nearby woods to find a certain magical plant guarded by a larger vermin-class monster.

3. Player tracks down and kills the King of Rats and finds the magical plant located conveniently in the King's corpse. Player comes back to the quest giver, who, in a cutscene, tries to use the plant to conjure up an astral gate in which he can summon help. The gate opens, but Something Evil reaches out, grabs the guy, and eats him whole. The last words of the quest giver are to send the player to the next town to warn the do-gooder there and to help to fight The Coming of Darkness.

Creating these types of quests is the staple of the designer of RPGs and will take up most of your time to script and ensure they are working. You may have to write some of the accompanying dialogue that goes with your quests, which may or may not get turned into voicelines depending on the importance of the scene.

Role-Playing Games with Editors

Dungeon Siege	Gas Powered Games	Microsoft
Morrowind	Bethesda Softworks	Bethesda Softworks
Neverwinter Knights	BioWare Corporation	Atari
Vampire: The Masquerade	Nihilistic Software	Activision, Inc.

Massively Multiplayer Online Role-Playing Games

The first and most important thing I think there is to know about designing MMOGs is that no two of them are really the same. From the engine to the tools to the final game, there are differences, some minor, some major, that make learning each one a brand-new experience. I've worked on three different MMOGs in the past four years, and all three of them were architected entirely differently. The tools are of course the main concern, but as almost every game out there uses proprietary tools, it's hard to go into detail on any specific set.

Instead, we'll take a little time to talk about the sorts of things you'll want to think about when designing for an MMOG. First of all, content has to be handled very differently. A majority of it is not going to be hit by the player just once. That player, as well as everyone else playing your game, will probably hit it multiple times. Making the content dynamic and able to handle multiple people using it at once is critical. What may seem like massive overkill for a single-player game may be just barely enough to keep your player base busy in a persistent universe. MMOGs do offer a lot of variety and opportunity in the design phases, from breadth and depth of content to multi-person quests and adventures of epic scale.

If you really want to mess around with a "persistent" universe without paying a few hundred thousand dollars in licensing fees, consider downloading the server and documentation for a popular MUD. There are a number of these freely available on the Web, and they could provide a good challenge, both technically and creatively, for the aspiring designer.

Note

MUDs, or *Multi-User Dungeons*, are the precursors to almost every major MMOG you can find on the market today. Almost every one of these were (and still are) text only, but you still had a persistent universe where many players could meet up and experience adventures together. Some very successful commercial MUDs are still available for play today, such as Dragonrealms and Gemstone.

Another good way to learn about MMOG development and even have a limited part in it is to become active in the community boards for games yet to be released. MMOGs are still a relatively new genre for the games industry, and many have very active communities, frequently with extensive community involvement from the developers themselves. A number of games still actively in development as of the writing of this book have already shown their willingness to communicate with their "fans" through public message boards and community events.

MMPORGs with Editors

Second Life   Linden Labs

Sports Games

Sports games tend to come in two types: super heroic and simulation.

- **Super heroic sports games** take an existing sport, like snowboarding or football, and empower its characters with abilities outstripping those of normal athletes to give it a more arcade-like feel.

- **Simulation sports games** attempt to recreate an actual sport to allow players to play out their athletic fantasies. These games rely on real-life statistics and licensing to allow their players maximum immersion.

For all sports games, the main focus is to recreate the feeling of the sport itself. This includes making sure that all the rules are fully explained and followed. The player is playing these games because he is very familiar with the sport, and he wants that familiarity to give him a feeling of competence.

Designing sports games requires a lot of knowledge of the sport you are working with. Not only knowledge of this past season, but the history of the sport as well can help you give your game that feeling of authenticity players are looking for. Being a baseball nut really helps when you are making baseball games, for instance.

There isn't much call for level designers on field sports games, like soccer, baseball, basketball, football, or tennis. There might be some effort to have the fields mimic their real-life counterparts, but there aren't really any placement or building duties that require an actual level designer.

Sports games that have variable fields, like skiing or skateboarding, can require level designers, as these fields generally aren't mimicking real-life areas, but are designed specifically for the player to do acrobatic tricks in as many unique and fun ways as possible. In these cases, a sense of flow around the field should be your biggest concern. Each jump or trick must flow smoothly into the approach for the next. Once the player masters the physical demands of the game, he will keep coming back because of that smooth flow of play.

Sports Games with Level Editors

Tiger Woods PGA Tour 2004 (PC)	Headgate Studios Inc.	EA Sports
Tony Hawk 3 + 4	Activision, Inc.	Activision, Inc.
Tony Hawks Underground, 1 & 2	Neversoft, Vicarious Visions	Activision, Inc.

Vehicle Simulations

People love their vehicles, whether they are boats, planes, cars, or trucks. They love them so much that there is a thriving business making programs that mimic a person's ability to use them.

Racing Games

Racing games come in two flavors: arcade and simulation.

- **Arcade racers** generally play fast and loose with the laws of physics, allowing players to jump farther, race faster, and drift better than a normal vehicle would be allowed. Arcade racers are primarily concerned with how fun it is to drive the car, and how fun it is to compete against other cars in races in exotic places or duplications of real-world tracks and locales.

- **Simulation racers** attempt to immerse the player by providing a real-world feeling to the cars. These games pay strict attention to simulating the physics that affect cars in real life, and only fudge when those physics make the cars completely undrivable. These types of games also give the player a large amount of freedom to tinker with the cars in the game, adjusting things like gear ratios and tire pressure to allow better performance in the game.

Design for racing games is firmly rooted in establishing systems. These systems determine how the mechanics interact with one another: how the cars work (and how the player's adjustments to the car's effects interact), how the AI responds when racing if they are too far ahead or behind, or how the player interacts with the game through the interface. Story is usually very limited in racing games, usually only taking place in cutscenes between races, if any.

Racing Games with Editors

TrackMania	Enlight Software	Nadeo
Hypersonic Xtreme (PS2)	Blade Interactive	Majesco

Flight Sims

Flight simulations are some of the most precise simulations available, so much so that some simulations can actually give the player registered flight time toward getting a pilot's license!

Design for flight sims is very systems oriented, detailing the interaction of the mechanics of the planes and the workings of the interface and AI.

Flight Simulators with Editors

Secret Weapons Over Normandy (PC)	Lawrence Holland and Totally Games	LucasArts Entertainment

Construction and Management Sims

Construction and management simulators have enjoyed a lot of popularity. Games like Maxis' *SimCity* and Frontier Development's *Rollercoaster Tycoon* allow players to be their own designers and create cities, zoos, rollercoasters, or a vast array of other constructs and systems for their own entertainment.

These types of games are not games at all really, but toolsets. In fact, a good way to begin your career as a designer is just to fool around with these games because they will familiarize you with the basics of how many mod-making and proprietary level design tools work.

Once again, because these games are simulations, the job of the designer lies mostly in creating different systems for the game. In a railroad sim, you might have to create a reward system for the player, figure out how railroads through the countryside differ from railroads through cities, or calculate how long it takes to build a railroad and how much virtual cash it takes to maintain it once it's there.

Adventure Games

Adventure games are games that rely heavily on story and puzzles to entertain the player. Not as popular as they once were, this genre of game is perhaps the most story-intensive of any type of game.

The design of adventure games relies heavily on the core story and the roadblocks you set up to prevent the player from getting through the story all at once. Here's an example of part of an adventure game:

> *Core Story*: The player finds himself in a lonesome village in the middle of an endless field of tall wheat. His car has broken down and he must ask the villagers for help so he can get to the large businessman's convention he was driving to in order to interview for a Big Job.
>
> At this point the player can go to any of the houses in the small town, but only a few people will answer his knock. When people answer the door, he asks if the occupant can help with his car problem, and is given the answer that he should go to the garage.
>
> The player eventually gets to the garage where the mechanic, Floyd, tells him he can fix his car. A cutscene happens where Floyd drags the player's car to the garage and looks under the hood. Floyd then approaches the player and says that he can't fix the car without a size 8 hose. He doesn't have one, but Fred, a farmer 20 miles down the road should have one for fixing his tractor. Floyd can't spend the time to drive the player to Fred's house, so the player will have to find his own way.
>
> The player now must find a way to Fred's. He sees some cars in the town, but he can't steal any… they are all locked. Through a process of elimination, he finds an elderly woman who owns an old car who will drive him to Fred's if the player can first help her flush a skunk out of her basement. However, if the player gets sprayed by the skunk, the old woman won't drive him anywhere, as she doesn't want the smell in her car.

This type of thing continues on, where the player, in order to succeed at his task, encounters roadblock after roadblock until he manages to complete the game.

Adventure games rely on great art as well as a great story to draw their audience. Lush backgrounds seeping with ambiance help immerse the player into the action of the game as much as the story does.

While there may not be any adventure games with editors to try your hand at creating them, there is a free toolset that will allow you to create your very own adventure game and an active community to share it with. Check it out at:

http://www.adventuregamestudio.co.uk/

Puzzle and Parlor Games

Puzzle and parlor games are very popular nowadays. Puzzle games, card games, board games, word games, and trivia games are driving millions of people to Web destinations like Zone.com and Pogo.com, as well as finding a place on handheld units like the Nintendo Gameboy DS and most cell phones.

Puzzle games rarely have any story attached to them, though their setting is usually very important to establishing a sense of identity. This identity is very important to puzzle games because the mechanics of these games tend to be fairly simple and can share elements with other puzzle games.

Puzzle games should always be easy to learn but hard to master, and should be repeatable and short.

The term "easy to learn but hard to master" is the Holy Grail of most games. It refers to games that a player can quickly understand the basic mechanics of, but must spend a long time learning the subtleties of before he can compete with the very best. Chess is my favorite example of this. It is pretty easy to pick up, but it requires a lifetime of study to compete at a grandmaster level.

Implementing this feature can be done in a variety of ways. You can create a difficulty ramp by increasing the challenge of the game as it goes on. This can be done by speeding up the pace of the game, or adding different challenges on top of the initial set. This is the easiest way to go about doing this.

A harder way to go is to allow the player a lot of freedom in what he can do. We'll use chess again for an example. Chess has a very large number of possible places a piece can be moved to. Having a game with this much freedom allows for many strategies, and thus a lot of depth. However, games like these are hard to program for AI, which is a major obstacle if you are trying to create a nice Internet game in Flash.

Puzzle games should also be repeatable. A game which one masters the first try through isn't much fun. The best of these games makes the player want to play the game again and again. Making the game challenging is a good way to make the game draw the player back for more (though, of course, too much challenge drives them away…), as will a good reward system.

Finally, puzzle games should be short. By this, I don't mean that the game should only last a few minutes, but that the player can complete a "round" of it in only a few minutes. This allows the player to quit easier, if he has to. It also speeds up the pace of the game, increasing the sense of challenge.

Some puzzle games don't need to be short, like jigsaw puzzles, for instance, but for Internet game play, fast-paced rounds are the way to go.

Technologically, simple Web games can be very easy to make. With widely available rapid development languages such as Macromedia Flash and Director, or even high-powered programming languages like Java, C#, and Visual Basic/ASP, the tools to make your game concept are easy to access, and have many tutorials and books available to help you learn how to create games in quick order.

Educational Games

Educational games, or edutainment, suffer a bad reputation in the game world for their sub-par graphics and simplistic gameplay. However, this genre, once constrained to software for children, is now growing rapidly into a fairly good business, creating games not only for kids, but also for large corporations that are using game-like environments to train their employees in a range of topics, from how to deal with sexual harassment to information management. Even the military uses game environments to teach their soldiers how to act in combat conditions.

Designing educational titles requires that you know the material to be trained, and have an idea of how to present that material as a set of rewards and punishments in a gaming atmosphere.

For instance, to train a person in how to deal with harassment in the workplace, you could create an adventure game where the player must make the correct responses to lewd remarks. For a factory line job, you could create a drag-and-drop game where the player must pull parts together in the correct order to make a virtual rendition of the robotic dog that the company is making out on the line.

As people everywhere become more and more familiar with video games, this type of training will become more popular. At some point in the future, they might become profitable enough to be able to afford the programmers and artists they need to compare favorably with more commercial games.

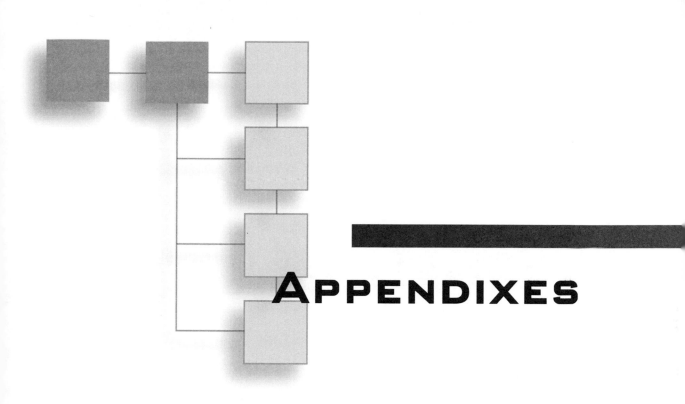

APPENDIXES

APPENDIX A

HELPFUL RESOURCES

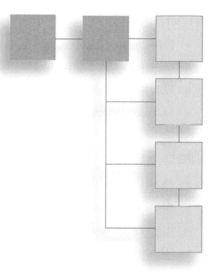

Because the game industry changes so rapidly, the most up-to-date resource will always be the Web itself. Type "game level design" into your favorite search engine for instant access to a wealth of information.

As of the writing of this edition (fall 2004), here are some of the best resources for game developers.

Game Design

- *Andrew Rollings and Ernest Adams on Game Design* by Andrew Rollings and Ernest Adams (New Riders, 2003)
- *The Art of Innovation* by Thomas Kelley (Doubleday, 2001)
- *Chris Crawford on Game Design* by Chris Crawford (New Riders, 2003)
- *Community Building on the Web* by Amy Jo Kim (Addison-Wesley, 2000)
- *Creating Emotion in Games* by David Freeman (New Riders, 2003)
- *Design of Everyday Things* by Donald A Norman (Basic Books, 2002)
- *Developing Online Games* by Jessica Mulligan and Bridgette Patrovsky (New Riders, 2003)
- *Game Architecture and Design: A New Edition* by Andrew Rollings and Dave Morris (New Riders, 2003)
- *Game Design: Secrets of the Sages* by Marc Saltzman (Bradygames, 1999)
- *Game Design: Theory and Practice* by Richard Rouse (Wordware, 2000)
- *Rules of Play* by Katie Salen and Eric Zimmerman (MIT Press, 2003)
- *Swords & Circuitry* by Neal and Jana Halford (Premier Press, 2001)

Magazines

- *Computer Graphics World* (cgw.com)
- *Game Developer Magazine* (gdmag.com)
- *Game Studies* (gamestudies.org)
- *Develop Magazine* (developmag.com)

Web Sites

- **avault.com/developer**
- **digitalgamedeveloper.com**
- **dperry.com/industry/index.htm**
- **flipcode.com**
- **gamasutra.com**
- **gamedev.net**
- **gameslice.com**
- **gametutorials.com**
- **gdse.com**
- **legendmud.org/raph/gaming/**

Conferences and Trade Shows

- **Anime Expo.** Japanese convention for fans of animation, comics, and pop culture.
- **Austin Game Conference.** Focuses on multiplayer and mobile games.
- **Australian Game Developers Conference.** Held annually in Melbourne, this conference is a mixture of keynotes, technical panels, and tutorials.
- **CES (Consumer Electronics Show).** U.S. trade show focusing on consumer electronics devices.
- **ChinaJoy.** Hong Kong digital entertainment expo & conference.
- **COMDEX.** U.S. trade show and conference for IT professionals.
- **Computational Semiotics for Games and New Media (COSIGN).** This European conference focuses on issues of meaning in new media, particularly the application of semiotic-based theories to creating and analyzing computer-based media.
- **DICE Summit.** U.S. single-track conference focused on "the creative endeavor inherent in game development."

- **Digifest.** Canadian festival of digital culture, creativity, and innovation.
- **Digital Games Research Conference.** European conference that bridges the academic research community and the professional gaming community.
- **E3.** The annual Electronic Entertainment Expo is the place to see all the games that are in development. If you don't currently work in the industry, you might have to pull some strings to get a pass. If you have a friend in the business, though, it's not difficult to arrange.
- **ECTS.** The European Computer Trade Show, held each fall in London, is like a European version of E3.
- **Eurographics Convention.** European conference for graphic artists.
- **GDC.** The Game Developers Conference is *the* place to meet other game developers, attend lectures on every possible subdiscipline of game development, and see all the latest development tools. If you can't afford to pay the registration fee, look into the conference associate position, which allows you to attend sessions for free in exchange for about 20 hours of volunteer work. Contact them at gdconf.com.
- **GDCE.** European version of the GDC, held each fall in London.
- **GCDC.** International Game Developer Conference, held each year in Leipzig, Germany.
- **Graphite.** International Conference on Computer Graphics and Interactive Techniques in Australasia and South East Asia.
- **MacWorld Conference & Expo.** Annual U.S. conference focused on the Macintosh OS.
- **MILIA.** Multimedia content event held each year in Cannes, France. Generally attended by executives, not the rank and file.
- **Project Bar-B-Q.** Unconventional annual Texas conference for industry musicians.
- **Shareware Industry Conference.** Three-day U.S. conference, culminating in the annual Shareware Industry Awards ceremony.
- **SIGGRAPH.** This is the premier annual U.S. gathering of artists interested in computer graphics.
- **3D Festival.** European event for 3D computer graphic artists.
- **Tokyo Game Show.** Japanese trade show & expo.
- **XGDX (EXtreme Game Developer's Xpo).** Annual two-day game development conference, held in Silicon Valley.

Industry News

- avault.com
- bluesnews.com
- escmag.com
- gamedaily.com
- gamesindustry.biz
- next-generation.com
- pc.ign.com/
- gamespot.com/

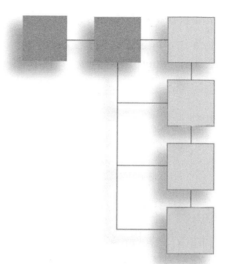

APPENDIX B

GLOSSARY

2D

Two-dimensional.

3D

Three-dimensional.

Actor

Common term used especially in first-person shooters or MMOGs to refer to Artificial Intelligences or NPCs. More descriptive, usually implies more complex behaviors.

AI

Artificial Intelligence.

Alpha, alpha testing

Alpha is an early stage of product development. Alpha testing is generally geared toward resolving gameplay issues.

Beta, beta testing

Beta is a late stage of product development, when the game is nearly complete. Beta testing generally focuses on finding and fixing bugs.

Boss

The hardest monster to kill in any given environment. He's usually encountered near the end of the level, after the player has dealt with all the "grunts."

Build

[Noun] The current version of the game.

[Verb] To assemble all subcomponents of the game into a working version.

CRPG

Computer Role-Playing Game. *See* RPG.

CTF

Capture The Flag. Multiplayer gaming mode.

Cutscene

A prerendered scene, usually shown between rounds of gameplay, that is designed to move the plot forward.

Deathmatch

Multiplayer gaming mode in which players battle each other head to head.

Developer

1.) A company with whom a publisher contracts to create the software for a game.

2.) An individual programmer, also known as a *coder*.

DevKit

Developer's Kit. A working prototype of a new console machine that's given to developers, so that they can make games for it before the actual hardware hits the market.

DGA

Directors Guild of America.

DirectMusic

A music delivery system developed by Microsoft for the PC.

Encounter

Term to describe any crafted event in the game, whether it be a puzzle, an individual to chat with, or a single/group of enemies to defeat.

Entity

See Actor.

Easter egg

A surprise feature or graphic, usually unrelated to gameplay, that's hidden in a game where most players won't find it. An unexpected bonus.

FMV

Full Motion Video. Filmed segments that are inserted into a game.

Foo

"Thing." What a game designer calls any unspecified object before he decides what it really is. Interchangeable with frob.

Frob

See foo.

Gantt chart

A time-based scheduling tool named for Henry Gantt, a pioneer of scientific management techniques.

GB

Gigabyte.

Going gold

Finishing development. (Sending the gold master off to be duplicated.)

Gold master

The master disc from which all other discs will be duplicated.

GUI

Graphical User Interface.

High concept

The one- or two-sentence response to the question, "What is your game about?"

Hit points

The amount of damage a weapon inflicts on its targets. Alternatively, the amount of damage a character or monster can absorb before it's disabled or killed.

HUD

Heads-Up Display. A portion of the screen that supplies crucial game-related information to the player.

IP

Intellectual Property.

1.) All the ideas, code, art, and other material your company develops.

2.) Shorthand for a franchise or brand you license to or from another company.

Isometric view

A "top-down" view that has a 3D appearance.

Lag

The amount of time it takes for information to travel over the Net. Also called *latency*.

LAN

Local Area Network.

Localization

The process of creating foreign-language versions of a game. The term covers a broad range of activities, including translating text, writing subtitles, dubbing voices, altering content that is deemed unsuitable for some markets, and creating new content altogether.

LOD

Level Of Detail. An algorithm that determines how many polygons to display as the player's distance from a model changes.

Maguffin

The object around which a story revolves. This word was coined by Alfred Hitchcock to describe an arbitrary device to keep a plot moving. In a game design, it refers to the most important item the gamer must acquire. In other words, it's the object of his quest.

MB

Megabyte.

MIDI

Musical Instrument Digital Interface. A standard that allows a composer to store and play music from data files rather than from recordings.

MMO, MMOG, MMP, MMORPG

Any acronym beginning with MM will be Massively Multiplayer. The O will stand for Online. The G will stand for Game. The P will be some variant of the word Play or Player.

Mocap

Motion capture.

MOD

Modification. A version of a popular game that has been changed or added to by the amateur gaming community.

Motion capture

An in-studio process whereby an actor's movements are digitally captured and transferred to a model in an animation program.

MP3

MPEG-3 (Moving Picture Experts Group Layer-3 Audio). A scheme to compress audio for quick transmission and easy playback.

MPEG

Moving Picture Experts Group. A video compression scheme that comes in two flavors, MPEG-1 and the higher-resolution MPEG-2.

NPC

Nonplayer Character. Any character appearing in a game that's not controlled by the gamer.

Objective

A fairly ambiguous term that refers to any goal, seen or unseen, for the player to accomplish in a level.

OEM

Original Equipment Manufacturer. Usually, a computer maker or a peripheral manufacturer who is interested in bundling your game with his hardware.

PERT chart

Program Evaluation and Review Technique. A project management tool that shows tasks and the dependencies between them.

Port

[Noun] A game version created for a different hardware platform than the original. Also called a *conversion*.

[Verb] To create such a conversion: "They ported the game from the PlayStation to the PC."

Powerup

An item that confers enhanced powers, usually found in action games.

Preproduction

The phase just prior to full development. The goal of preproduction is to create a full set of design documents and a proof-of-concept piece of technology.

Price protection

The lowering of a game's wholesale price. Usually, this comes in the form of a credit to the retailer for units he has on the shelves but hasn't sold through. The markdown is taken as the game's rate of sales slows down, to encourage the retailer to keep the game in stock rather than return it to the publisher.

Redbook audio

A fancy name for the digital standard developed by Phillips and Sony to record the regular CDs that go in your stereo. So called because the original specification was in a book with a red binder.

RPG

Role-Playing Game. A genre in which the player directs a group of heroes on a series of quests, usually in a story-based environment.

RTM

Release To Manufacture. The point at which development stops and the gold master is shipped off for duplication. Also known as *going gold*.

RTS

Real-Time Strategy. A genre of games played in real time (as opposed to turn-based games), in which the player must manage a limited set of resources to achieve a goal.

SDK

Software Development Kit. A set of technologies that allows a programmer to create applications for a particular platform.

Scripting

Catch-all term to refer to enhancing or extending the gameplay of a level through the use of code/special tools.

Sell-in

The number of units a publisher places in the retail channel.

Sell-through

The number of units that are actually sold at retail.

Showstopper

A bug that's important enough to hold up the release of a game.

Storyboard

[Noun] A sequence of pencil sketches that rough out what a scene will look like.

[Verb] To create this sequence.

Studio

1.) An independent development house (or *developer*) that develops game software.

2.) A division of a large company that acts as a semi-autonomous unit to develop games.

3.) A soundproof room for recording actors' voices, also known as a *voice studio*.

4.) An interior location for filming.

SWAG

See WAG.

Trigger

Something defined in the level, usually an invisible "box" or shape that's placed on the landscape to let the game engine know when something has happened, such as a player entering or exiting.

UBG

Ultimate Bad Guy. What a game designer calls the villain in the early stages of design, before his identity has been developed.

UI

User Interface.

WAG

Wild-Ass Guess. Off-the-cuff estimate. Sometimes SWAG, or Scientific (or Silly) Wild-Ass Guess.

WAN

Wide Area Network.

WIP

Work In Progress. Often attached to an asset's name to indicate that it's not yet final.

WYSIWYG

What You See Is What You Get. Any interface that allows you to see what the material will look like on the computer screen while you're creating it.

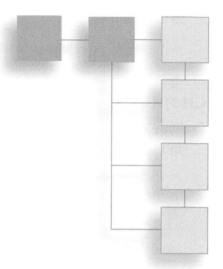

APPENDIX C

REVIEW QUESTIONS AND ANSWERS

In this appendix you will find the review questions and answers from each chapter.

Chapter 1

1. As a game maker, your primary duty is to do what?

    A: *Entertain people.*

2. What are the three types of power?

    A: *Creative, Destructive, and Manipulative.*

3. Where can you go to find opinions and thoughts about games so you can find out what works and what doesn't?

    A: *Game reviews, internet message boards, game-related Websites and magazines.*

4. Name three types of challenges:

    A: *Time Challenge, Dexterity Challenge, Endurance Challenge, Memory/Knowledge Challenge, Cleverness/Logic Challenge, Resource control Challenge.*

5. What is hubris?

A: *Overbearing pride or presumption.*

Chapter 2

1. Why should you bother to put your game idea on paper, instead of going right to the level editor and cranking it out?

A: *Putting your ideas on paper allows you to see them in a new light. It reveals all the inconsistencies and logical disconnects.*

2. How do I come up with great ideas?

A: *A great idea generally starts as a bad idea that some stubborn person continues to think about until it becomes great. Any idea can be great if you refine it enough. It may not look like your original idea after you're done, but you'll like it better, I promise.*

3. What is a storyboard?

A: *A storyboard is a sequence of still images that show what will happen in a proposed animated sequence, such as a movie or cartoon. In game design, storyboards are used to show what will happen in a cutscene. Level designers can also use storyboards or comic strips to show the sequence of events in a level.*

4. What is a topographical map?

A: *A topographical map shows the surface features of the terrain, usually as elevation data. This is useful for showing rugged terrain in games.*

Chapter 3

1. How does a heightmap work?

A: *A heightmap uses the 256 shades of gray in a black-and-white digital picture to remember surface features. Each shade of gray represents a certain elevation. Black is the lowest possible elevation, and white is the highest.*

2. What's frustrating to a player?

   a) Invisible walls
   b) A lack of landmarks
   c) Not being able to see his opponent
   d) All of the above

   A: *d) All of the above.*

3. Name three ways that terrain can be fun.

   A: *It can be fun to move around on, it can tell a story, and it can generate suspense.*

4. What are some of the things you have to consider when texturing your terrain?

   A: *Whether the textures are appropriate to the scenario you're working on, and whether they look good (no seams, not stretched because of sudden elevation changes, no obviously repeated squares).*

5. What are some of the things you have to consider when placing props on your terrain?

   A: *Whether the props are appropriate to the scenario, whether they look like clones of each other, and whether they interfere with the gameplay of the level.*

Chapter 4

1. Why wouldn't a level that perfectly duplicates an average living room be fun for players?

   A: *Because of the speed at which game characters run, and the fact that they run all the time, a normally furnished living room would be very frustrating to navigate.*

2. How do architects encourage movement of people from one space to another within a building?

   A: *By the use of corners, which push people away, and open spaces, which pull people toward them, an architect can encourage the flow of people from one room to another.*

3. Why is texturing architecture more difficult than texturing terrain?

A: *The sheer number of textures in a building outnumbers the simpler textures in terrain. Plus, many special textures, like transparent and reflective textures, are abundant in architecture.*

4. Name some standard features of a building in a fantasy genre game.

A: *Thick stone walls, a lava pool in the backyard, suits of armor hanging out in the halls, etc.*

5. In what type of game would it be fun to have a building based on a painting by M.C. Escher?

A: *Games devoted to solving mysteries or puzzles. Architecture like this wouldn't be fun in any type of game that requires ease of movement, like a fast deathmatch level.*

Chapter 5

1. What two types of lights are available to use in games?

A: *Static and dynamic lights.*

2. What are the three forms each light may take?

A: *Point lights, directed lights, and spotlights.*

3. Name three types of particle effects.

A: *Choose from: water spritzing, swarms of insects, dust motes, flocks of geese, etc.*

4. Name the three senses for which games provide stimulus.

A. *Sight, hearing, and touch.*

5. Why is fog good for your game?

A. *It reduces the number of objects the game has to draw.*

Chapter 6

1. When choosing a spawn point for the player, what type of location would you look for?

   a) A location where the player can see and understand his first objective.

   b) A place where the player won't be immediately attacked.

   c) Both a and b.

   d) None of the above.

   A: *C*

2. Name a type of formation.

   A: *Wedge, column, or echelon.*

3. Why is spawning an enemy better than having him exist from the moment the level is loaded?

   A: *It saves processor time if the enemy isn't around until he's needed.*

4. What is a spawn point?

   A: *A position in a game where an object can be created.*

5. What is bloodlocking?

   A: *When a player has to kill x things in order to progress beyond a certain point in a level or game.*

6. What is an informational encounter?

   A. *An encounter whose sole purpose is to inform the player.*

Chapter 7

1. What is a script?

    A: *A small program that allows the designer to control a given aspect of the game.*

2. What types of things can a script control?

    A: *Dialogue, movement, spawn rate, environmental conditions, game world physics, and character statistics are a few examples.*

3. When building a quest for a game, what elements should you expect to have to plan for/implement?

    A: *Flags, conversations, scripts to evaluate flags, actors to provide or finish the quest.*

4. What types of objects, moving or otherwise, could you add to an abandoned military base to give it more life and flavor?

    A: *Elevators, a crashed helicopter, mutated guards on patrol, smoke coming out of a seemingly abandoned building, animals roaming the more overgrown parts of the structure.*

Chapter 8

1. What are the two main differences between stories for games and stories for movies or novels?

    A: *Games have a non-linear nature that makes it hard to tell sequential stories. Games are also interactive, so the main character (the player) won't always do exactly what your story wants him to do.*

2. What clues does Maslow's hierarchy of needs give in telling stories in games?

    A: *Players find stories the least of their concern when faced with having to learn things such as using the interface and keeping themselves safe from danger.*

3. All voicelines should have the same two qualities. What are they?

    A: *Voicelines should be short and informative.*

4. What are the six aspects of any plot?

    A: *Who, when, where, what, why, and how.*

5. A games relies mostly on what to tell the player its story?

    A: *Characters.*

6. Who is the most important character to develop in your game?

    A: *The villain.*

7. What are voicelines?

    A: *Voicelines are the computer files where dialogue is stored. When you want a character to say something, you launch a voiceline.*

8. How long should in-game voicelines be?

    A: *Between 7 and 11 seconds is best.*

9. What is a conversation tree?

    A: *A conversation tree is a method of communication in games whereby the player is presented with a menu of conversational lines and questions in order to inter- act with an NPC.*

Chapter 9

1. What is the key to having a solid game?

    A: *Iteration. Playing it over and over helps you find the bumps and smooth them over.*

2. What is the difference between free testing and planned testing?

    A: *Free testing allows the tester to test whatever he wants, but can leave gaps and, if there are a lot of free testers, can encourage overlap, which is a waste of time. Planned testing uses a test plan to direct the tester's efforts, but can suffer from a lack of creativity that misses interesting and crazy bugs.*

3. What is an "A" bug?

    A: *A bug that prevents the player from completing the game.*

4. If you see a gap in your terrain, what should you do to try and fix it?

    A: *Have the engine rebuild the terrain. If it still has problems, try smoothing the sharp edges around the gap.*

5. If you have a normal problem, how should you go about fixing it?

    A: *Block it from view, or replace it with a 2-sided object.*

6. Name the three most common problems that cause scripts not to work.

    A: *Misspellings, incorrectly placed or extra punctuation, and incorrect cases in letters.*

7. Why is it important to have another person test your level?

    A: *The designer gets too close to the game and can no longer be objective.*

Appendix D

What's on the CD

The attached CD is where you'll find all the example *Far Cry* levels we used to demonstrate each chapter's focus. To view and run these files, you'll need Ubisoft's *Far Cry* game. We've also included a link to the *Far Cry* Web site, where you can download their excellent manual as well as the *Far Cry* SDK, if you really want to go wild.

Here's a listing of what you'll find, broken down by chapter.

Chapter 3
Prospero's Island with textured terrain and vegetation.

Chapter 4
Prospero's Island, now with rooms inside the hill and an elevator shaft.

Chapter 5
Lighting added to interior rooms.

Chapter 6
Creatures placed on map.

Chapter 7
Added scripts for mission requirements and elevator action.

Chapter 9
Bug fixes, changes to the sky and overall lighting, and less vegetation.

Feel free to augment, experiment, and play with these levels to your heart's content.

INDEX